THE ADVENTURES OF MY GRANDFATHER.

WITH EXTRACTS FROM HIS LETTERS, AND OTHER FAMILY DOCUMENTS, PREPARED FOR THE PRESS WITH NOTES AND BIOGRAPHICAL SKETCHES OF HIMSELF AND HIS SON, JOHN HOWE PEYTON, ESQ.

BY

JOHN LEWIS PEYTON, L.L.B., F.R.G.S.

Author of " The American Crisis," " A Historical and Statistical View of the State of Illinois."
Late Chief of Staff to General Douglas B. Layne of Virginia.

"Ἄριστοι ἀκμάς
οὐ σκολιῶν μύθων ἄμμες ἐφιέμεθα

LONDON:
JOHN WILSON, PUBLISHER,
93, GREAT RUSSELL STREET, W.C.

MDCCCLXVII.

[All rights reserved]

In the interest of creating a more extensive selection of rare historical book reprints, we have chosen to reproduce this title even though it may possibly have occasional imperfections such as missing and blurred pages, missing text, poor pictures, markings, dark backgrounds and other reproduction issues beyond our control. Because this work is culturally important, we have made it available as a part of our commitment to protecting, preserving and promoting the world's literature. Thank you for your understanding.

To

SIR STAFFORD CAREY,

THE BAILIFF OF GUERNSEY,

AN ABLE LAWYER AND UPRIGHT JUDGE,

This Volume

IS INSCRIBED,

WITH FEELINGS OF SINCERE ADMIRATION AND RESPECT,

BY

HIS FRIEND,

J. LEWIS PEYTON.

Reform Club, Pall Mall,
October 28, 1867.

ADVERTISEMENT.

This volume consists of three parts. The first comprises the Life of my Grandfather, with a selected portion of his Correspondence, detailing what may be termed his adventures. Many of the Papers which came into my hands as the executor of my father, including letters written by himself, his father, and other members of the family, having been burnt or mutilated during the Civil War in America, I have had some difficulty in connecting together in the form of a narrative the following imperfect series of letters by my grandfather. In order to do this with tolerable success, I have been under the necessity, in cases where the meaning appeared tolerably clear, of supplying a few lines to fill the hiatus. If this should, in any instance, have caused obscurity or anachronism, I hope this will be a sufficient explanation, especially as it has arisen from a strong wish to render the narrative not only agreeable to my family, for whose gratification it is specially designed, but interesting to the public. I am far from being confident that much success has attended my efforts; I trust, however, that too much will not be expected, in regard to literary execution, from one whose life has been principally devoted to active pursuits and the service of his country, and that this fact will compensate for many blemishes in style and arrangement. I am indebted to the courtesy of the Bailiff of Guernsey for the perusal of an interesting manuscript account of the siege of Carthagena, written by his kinsman, Captain John Stafford, who left his residence in Virginia to take part in that Expedition. This manuscript has fortunately enabled me to supply some names, dates, and items in the three first letters of my grandfather. The second part of this volume consists of a brief biographical sketch of my father; and the third is a narrative of the circumstances attending the settlement in Virginia of my maternal ancestors, a family of Norman Huguenots, which took refuge in Scotland from the persecutions to which Protestants were subjected in France after the Revocation of the Edict of Nantes. The contents of each part are given separately, and in the order which exhibits most naturally the connection of the subjects.

J. L. P.

CONTENTS.

CHAPTER I.

                                                                                                         Page.

Preliminary Biographical Sketch of my Grandfather—His Birth, Parentage and Early School Days.   1

CHAPTER II.

He commences his University Career.—Letter from his Father.—His reception at Williamsburg.—Fashionable Customs in the Capital.—His continued success as a Scholar.—Colonel Bland.   13

CHAPTER III.

He visits New York.—Is Shipwrecked on the Return Voyage.—His account of the Affair.—He commences the Study of Military Engineering and the Art of War under Colonel De Blois in Richmond.   23

CHAPTER IV.

He leaves Richmond and returns to Stoney Hill.—Sails for the West Indies.—His account of the Voyage.—Sickness on Board the Vessel.—Scarcity of Water.—Storm off the North Carolina Coast.—Sight the French Keys.—Lands at Titchfield and dines with the President.   29

Contents.

CHAPTER V.

Some account of Scenery and Natural Productions of Jamaica.—The Slaves.—A Sugar Plantation.—Bad Husbandry.—A Negro Device for taking Fish.—Fruits and Flowers.—Mountain Roads.—Captain Pelham, R.E.—Spanish Town.—Entertainment by the Governor.—Unexpected Meeting with a Party of Virginians.—Society in Jamaica. 37

CHAPTER VI.

He visits Carthagena.—City and Bay.—Churches.—Popular Ignorance and Superstition.—The Siege of 1741.—Death of his Uncle.—A North Carolinian.—Returns to Jamaica.—Annie Howe, the Bright Particular Star of Spanish Town.—Brief account of Jamaica conceived in the Right Spirit. . . 46

CHAPTER VII.

He sails for New Orleans.—The Mississippi River.—New Orleans.—The Inhabitants.—Historical Coup d'Œil.—General D'Uloa.—Count O'Reilly.—Judicial Murders and Confiscations.—The Governor and his Entertaiment. 55

CHAPTER VIII.

He sails for Florida but is captured by the Spaniards and carried to New Mexico.—Marches eighty-nine days up the Rio del Norte to Santa Fé, where he is imprisoned and treated with Inhuman Barbarity. 63

CHAPTER IX.

Mr. Howe visits England in Pursuit of Legal Business.—Secures a Great Success.—Forms the Acquaintance of an Amicus Curia.—Jimmy Jones.—Returns to Jamaica to find his Wife furious and his Daughter in Love.—The Family at Home on the Occoquan in Virginia. 82

CHAPTER X.

Absent but not forgotten.—A Rival in the Field.—Captain Pelham in a New Character. 96

Contents.

CHAPTER XI.

He resumes his letter from St. Louis.—His Escape from the Santa Fé Prison and Flight across the Rocky Mountains.—Traverses the Great Plains of the Interior of North America and arrives in St. Louis guided by an Osage Warrior. . . 103

CHAPTER XII.

Third and Last Letter from St. Louis.—He meets a Virginian who supplies his wants.—Marriage of his Valet with Annetta Ximenes.—Indian Hostilities in Illinois, Indiana and Ohio.—Description of Santa Fé and the Plains. . . . 115

CHAPTER XIII.

He arrives at the Mouth of the Kentucky River.—Democratic Sentiments in the Backwoods Settlement.—Visit to an Indian Town.—Mammoth Bones.—Antiquities.—Aspect of the Country.—Defeat of a French and Indian Force by the Chickasaws. 124

CHAPTER XIV.

He arrives on the Great Kenewha River.—Meets and joins the Army of General Lewis.—Takes part in the Battle of Point Pleasants.—Account of the Battle and Sketch of General Lewis and of the Lamented Colonel Charles Lewis.—Is wounded and removed to the Greenbrier. 131

CHAPTER XV.

He leaves the Warm Springs.—Mountain Scenery.—Beautiful Cascade.—Legend.—Arrives at Staunton and proceeds to Norfolk.—The Political Agitations preceding the American Revolution. 149

CHAPTER XVI.

Letter from John Peyton, Esq. to John Rowzée Peyton, Esq. . 160

CHAPTER XVII.

His return to Stoney Hill.—Political Agitation preceding the American Revolution. 163

CHAPTER XVIII.

His Marriage.—The Festivities.—Captain Pelham Redivivus.—Mr. Jimmy Jones in Character.—Death of the Venerable John Peyton.—His Character.—Concluding Remarks. . . 167

Biographical Sketch of John Howe Peyton, Esq. of Montgomery Hall, Augusta County, Virginia. 181
Sketch of a Distinguished Lawyer 205
Narrative of the Circumstances connected with the Settlement of M. Jean Louis, or John Lewis, and his Family in Virginia . 215

APPENDIX.

John Peyton, Esq., to his cousin Henry Peyton, Esq. . . 227
John Peyton, Esq., to his cousin, Henry Peyton, Esq. . . 233
John Peyton, Esq., to his cousin, Henry Peyton, Esq. . . 236
Captain Francis Peyton to his Mother 240

THE ADVENTURES OF MY GRANDFATHER.

CHAPTER I.

PRELIMINARY BIOGRAPHICAL SKETCH OF MY GRANDFATHER.—HIS BIRTH, PARENTAGE AND EARLY SCHOOL DAYS.

THE subject of this sketch, John Rowzée Peyton, was born May 16th, 1752, at "Stoney Hill,"* Stafford County, Virginia, and was the son of John Peyton, Esquire, by his wife, Elizabeth Rowzée, of the County of Essex.

His father was a lineal descendant of Robert Peyton, of Isleham, in the county of Mathews, Virginia, the first of the family who emigrated to America. Robert was the grandson of the Puritan and Cromwellian partizan, Sir Edward Peyton, Knight and Baronet, the author of a very curious, equally bitter, and, in all probability, perfectly veracious history of the court and cabinet of James I.† At the Restoration, Robert Peyton settled in Virginia, where he named his residence Isleham, in

---

* The family seat in Virginia.

† Sir Edward Peyton suffered extensive losses during the civil war, only retaining a life interest in Isleham of a few hundreds a year, which were necessary to supply the expenses of a gentleman. He does not appear to have recovered any thing at the hands of Cromwell though he hastened to arm his tenantry & melt his hereditary plate in the service of the Parliamentarians. vide Sir Bernard Burkes Extraordinary Baronetcies head "Peyton of Isleham", also the Introd. to

memory of his ancestral English home, and where his offspring continue, after the lapse of two centuries, verifying, in their high position and worldly prosperity, the words of the Psalmist, "I have been young and now am old, yet never saw I the virtuous man forsaken, nor his seed begging their bread." His mother belonged to a French Protestant family, which fled from France to Scotland after the revocation of the edict of Nantes. From Scotland they removed to Oporto in Portugal, and, finally, to North America. They, too, are among the principal gentry of Virginia.

We have thought it not out of place to enter thus briefly upon his pedigree, which, if traced, will be seen to be not only conspicuous by rank and wealth, but by the superior lustre of virtue.

He gave early tokens of more than ordinary promise, both as to moral qualities and intellectual endowments. His parents regarded him, therefore, with singular affection, and determined to improve his natural parts by the best education to be acquired in the colony at that early day. As there were no schools nearer than Dumfries, they engaged a private tutor. By the advice of a friend, they secured the services, in this capacity, of Mr. Buchan, a Scotch emigrant, at that time residing in the town of Falmouth. Mr. Buchan was described as a man of extensive and varied erudition, of excellent judgment, and unexceptionable manners and habits; and, moreover, thoroughly devoted to the task of educating and rearing the young. This worthy man came to America some years previous, as tutor to the son of Lord Fairfax.

of Elizabeth & King James" by Francis Osborne Esq.r which were reprinted in 2 vols: at Edinborough in 1811 — printed by James Ballantyne & Co. In which work is a reprint of "The Divine Catastrophe of the King's family of the house of Stuarts; or a short history of the rise, reign, & ruine thereof" &c. Sir Edward Peyton, Knight & Baronet

Mr. Buchan took up his residence at Stoney Hill, May, 1760, and remained there in the discharge of his duties for the next three years. During this period, the progress of his pupil was entirely satisfactory, and his father determined to enter him at a boarding school shortly to be opened in the neighbouring town of Dumfries. He was particularly inclined to take this course, as Mr. Buchan had accepted a situation as junior head-master in the new seminary.

Dumfries was, at this period, the most flourishing town in that section of Virginia, a port of entry where the planters received their supplies, principally from England, and from which they shipped their corn and tobacco—the two most important staples of Virginia then as now. For mutual benefit, the neighbouring gentry determined to establish, in this central point, the public school to which we have just referred.

Dumfries has long ceased to be a place of the slightest importance. The few houses now standing are strongly expressive of poverty and squalid wretchedness. It has been completely engulfed in the prosperity of its rival, Fredericksburg.* A few crumbling brick chimneys, some scattered ruins, draped with ivy and the Virginia creeper, and a half hundred tumble-down buildings, are all that remain of the gay shops and comfortable residences, and the long lines of wooden warehouses, where the crops of the colonial planters were once stored. One can scarcely, when viewing the present wreck, credit the accounts of its early grandeur and opulence, but nothing is truer than

* Since so famous in the annals of the Civil War.

that Dumfries was anciently a most flourishing city. Its present inferiority and decay is the result of departed commerce — commerce, that fluctuating will-o'-the-wisp that only leads states after it, to entrap them ultimately into mires and precipices, and which, when caught, stays till it extinguishes the spirit of liberty in a nation, refines its people into feeble slaves, and there leaves them to poverty and contempt.

Perhaps there is no subject that affords an ampler field for a speculative mind to expatiate upon, than the various, and we may say, incongruous revolutions which have chequered the progress of human society from the first records of history down to the present time. It is, indeed, a speculation which not only tends to improve the understanding, by calling in experience to correct the illusions of theory, but is highly instructive in a moral point of view, by pointing out the instability of the very best structures of human wisdom, and teaching us how little reliance is to be placed upon human casualties or earthly contingencies.

It was due to this irresistible mutation of things, that Dumfries sank from its high condition to its present low estate. In the days of which we write, it boasted a tobacco exchange, a chamber of commerce, a post-office, a newspaper, a double row of shops, where the last English importations were displayed to the best advantage. It was also the head-quarters of the farmers and planters club, which assembled in a room of the principal inn, a public-house which had risen since the close of the last French war, upon the ruins of the "Royal George."

In the club-room of this inn the county gentlemen assembled daily to interchange views upon agriculture and politics, and to digest the gossip of the community. Dumfries was, indeed, a kind of news mart, as well as commercial capital, where everything passing in the general assembly at Williamsburg (the colonial capital) was sure to be thoroughly canvassed over roast beef and Jamaica rum. It was also an assize town, where the circuit judge and public prosecutor made their periodical appearances to the terror of evil doers; and the seat of a number of primary schools. It had now also become the distinguished seat of a public academy. Those were the palmy days of Dumfries, and Mr. Buchan, who was one of the two heads, and by no means the least important, under which the infant seat of academic learning was launched, was in his glory also.

The subject of this sketch was entered as a pupil in this academy. As may be imagined, it was a period of great excitement with him, and anxiety to his parents; with him at the prospect of giving up the seclusion of an old Virginia home, and his father's at Stoney Hill, which was built, after the style of an English country mansion of the Inigo Jones architectural school, of brick brought from England, in combination with the native sand stone, and surrounded with extensive grounds, improved after the manner of the parks, for which the mother country is so famous; was the home of taste, refinement, and luxury, where he had always been contented and happy. All the associations of his youth were connected with this spot, and his heart saddened at the prospect of leaving it—even for the more active and exciting life of a public school. His parents, too, were full of anxious solicitude lest he might fall into temptation and stray from the paths of temperance and virtue, of sobriety and study in this sink of iniquity, as they pictured to themselves Dumfries with its score of sea-going vessels, its few dozen fishing smacks, and its occasional crowds of sailors and strangers. Their apprehensions were great too, lest he should not maintain upon this new theatre, and when brought in competition with a select and numerous body of boys of talent, the high reputation he had already acquired for cleverness and progress.

Whatever were their feelings of anxiety, he was fetched at the appointed time in the family chariot, and deposited as a boarder at the house of the head-master. Here he was left by his parents with many a fervent prayer, and many a godly admonition to beware of the alluring temptations to which he should be exposed, and many an exhortation to be dutiful in his conduct to his superiors, and assiduous in his studies. He was supplied with a bible, and the scant stock of text books then in vogue in Virginia, consisting of an elementary treatise on geography, another on arithmetic, and the works for juniors in Latin and Greek.

As regards the manner in which he was bred up by his parents, previous to entering the school at Dumfries, he was often heard in after years to speak in grateful terms, to the effect that his infant reason no sooner dawned, than they began to use every possible means to give that reason a right bias towards its proper object ; that they daily approached the throne of grace with fervent prayer for their helpless children, before these children knew how to pray for themselves. He said he had often stood at the door, while a rude unthinking boy, of his pious grandmother's closet, and heard many heart-affecting groans and ardent supplications poured forth for himself. While many of the neighbouring gentry seemed rather to inculcate in the minds of their children the love of sinful pleasures and perishing vanities, his endeavoured to persuade him to a love of God and the pursuit of eternal things. A religious education will not certainly always restrain the vicious inclinations of youth, but it is, nevertheless, a means of grace from which many have reaped the greatest advantage. Sooner or later the assiduous labours of such parents will be rewarded, and he was an evidence of this truth. Through life, he constantly gave proofs of the virtuous principles he had imbibed in his youth, and the pious examples constantly set before his eyes. He often remarked in after life that it was his careful home training which gave him self-respect, when brought in contact with the world, and preserved him from any taste for low and vicious society or indulgences. One important feature of his home influence was his father's habit of reading aloud. Regarding reading as one great means of mental improvement, in connection with good literary training, it was his custom to read aloud to his family several hours every evening. It gave his children a relish for good books, and was to them as to him, a constant source of happiness and cheerfulness through life. His remarks upon this subject have vividly recalled the words of Herschel, " If I were to pray for a taste which should stand me under every variety of circumstances, it would be a taste for reading. I speak of it, of course, only as a worldly advantage, and not in the slightest degree derogating from the higher office, and sure and stronger panoply of religious principles, but as a taste, an instrument, and a mode of pleasurable gratification. Give a man this taste, and the means of gratifying it, and you can hardly fail of making him a happy man, unless, indeed, you put into his hands a most perverse selection of books. You place him in contact with the best society in every period of history, with the wisest, the wittiest, with the tenderest, the bravest, and the purest characters who have adorned humanity. You make him a denizen of all nations, a contemporary of all ages. The world has been created for him.

"It is hardly possible but the character should take a higher and better tone from this constant habit of associating in thought with a class of thinkers, to say the least of it, above the average of humanity. It is morally impossible but that the manners should take a tinge of good breeding and civilization, from having constantly before our eyes the way in which the best bred and best informed men have talked and conducted themselves in their intercourse with each other. There is a gentle but perfectly irresistible coercion in a habit of reading, well directed, over the whole tenor of a man's character and conduct, which is not the least effectual because it works insensibly, and because it is really the last thing he dreams of. It cannot be better summed up than in the words of the Latin poet: "*Emollit mores, nec sinit esse feros!*" It civilizes the conduct of men, and suffers them not to remain barbarous."

He thus acquired a tolerable knowledge of history before he was twelve years of age, and astonished his school-fellows with his conversation about Leonidas and Aristides, Cyrus and Xerxes, Alexander and Hannibal, Scipio and Cato, and a host of other ancient worthies, who stood before him, living, breathing men, whom he loved and hated, whose conquests or defeats made his heart glow with delight, or burn with indignation! The result of his early and careful home training was obvious in his whole career, and by friend and foe alike, (if he had enemies), down to the latest period of his life, he was regarded as a man of perfect probity, of the highest honour, an honour which amounted to a scruple, and of an uprightness of heart which was proof against corruption. Some remarkable evidences of this fact were disclosed after his death by his private papers. Among them was found a violent letter written to him from Fredericksburg in 1790, by the late William Charles Fenton of Roanoke, complaining that Mr. Peyton had directed an action at law to be instituted against him without having previously asked an explanation which might have resulted in an adjustment of the difficulty. Before closing a long letter, setting forth his grievance, Mr. Fenton added these remarkable words, "I do not wish to be misunderstood. I do not intend to charge that you have intentionally done me wrong, or I should rather say had any intention of wronging me by this course—far be it from me to assail your honour or integrity. Notwithstanding the position you occupy in this affair, my unhandsome treatment, I believe you as honest a man as lives."

Some years after Mr. Peyton's death, his son met Mr. Fenton in Fredericksburg, where he happened to be on a casual visit, having, years before, migrated to the State of Louisiana, and mentioned to him the fact of finding this letter, and asked an explanation of the circumstances of exasperation under which it seemed to have been written. Mr. Fenton immediately smiled, and taking the young man by the hand, said—"Think no more of the affair. I was wrong from beginning to end, and wrote the letter in a moment of petulance, and so told your father afterwards, thus making the *amende honorable*; and our old friendship was not disturbed."

Except during the annual school vacations, he passed four years in Dumfries Academy, during which period he acquired a thorough knowledge of Greek and Latin, and made astonishing progress in mathematics, for which his talent was peculiar, intuitive, amounting to what may be termed a genius for it. At this time he was withdrawn from the school, to be entered at the University of "William and Mary," situated near Williamsburg, the colonial capital of Virginia. "William and Mary" was, at that period, the most famous of all the American institutions of learning. At the epoch of his transfer to the University, he was the acknowledged leader of the Academy in every department of knowledge comprised in the scholastic course of study, having not only maintained the good opinion expressed of his capacity by his tutor, but exceeded the most sanguine expectations formed of his abilities. The following are

the circumstances under which he was about to proceed to
" William and Mary."

His father said to him upon one occasion, about this
period (1765), when on a visit to Stoney Hill—

" 1 am already the father of six children, and my young
family is growing. Though one of, what we call, the
wealthy planters of the country, I foresee that I shall not
be able to make any large settlement for my children.
They must, in a great measure, depend upon their own
exertions for success in life. You have already made some
progress in your education—quite enough to pass cur-
rently among our Virginian planters, and make a figure in
the Legislature. If you are disposed now to go to work
in the direction of agriculture, I will settle upon you my
Clermont estate, with a sufficient force of slaves to enable
you to live in ease and independence, and to bring up a
family respectably; but if you wish to continue your
education at a university and to enter the Church, to
study physic, or follow the law, I am willing to supply you
with the means to any proper extent you may wish, but
these advances must be subtracted from the present value
of the property which I am willing and able to advance
you by way of settlement. You ought to know at once
what your mind is upon such a subject, but I wish you to
reflect over it, and give me your decision to-morrow."

He immediately said to his father—

" I do not require till to-morrow to give you answer. I
have a fixed choice and determination, and have arrived at
it after reflection : it is to continue my education at the
University, and to follow the profession of arms in the

service of my sovereign. It adds, however, to my affectionate veneration and respect for a kind parent that you have spoken so candidly, and given me the option of two courses, under such circumstances. I abandon all interest in your estate, beyond a few hundreds a-year, in favour of my brothers and sisters, and only ask to be prepared by academic and professional education to take my proper place in society and in my profession."

It would hardly have been suspected that his inclinations were in the direction of the army, for at this period he is known to have suffered from a constitutional reserve and a delicate sensibility which was frequently offended at the rudeness of the masters in speaking to his schoolfellows. He often went so far as to say to Mr. Buchan and others, that " it was not the way to do a boy good to wound his feelings." It was a remarkable trait in his character at this time, as indeed through life, that he never expressed himself censoriously or contemptuously of those who by conscientious investigation, were led to different conclusions from himself. Nevertheless, he frequently enlivened his conversation by a vein of wit bordering on satire. His individual character had been gradually and silently developing amid these influences. He had grown up into a tall, vigorous lad of sixteen, full of animal spirits, and full, too, of the restlessness of a boy's nature. This restless activity was chiefly expended in the prosecution of his studies, in the acquisition of knowledge. He felt within the stirrings of that mysterious spirit which told him that God gave us not

"That capability and god-like reason
To rust in us unused."

CHAPTER II.

HE COMMENCES HIS UNIVERSITY CAREER.—LETTER FROM HIS FATHER.—HIS RECEPTION AT WILLIAMSBURG.—FASHIONABLE CUSTOMS IN THE CAPITAL. —HIS CONTINUED SUCCESS AS A SCHOLAR.—COLONEL BLAND.

HAVING passed his vacation at home, he proceeded to make his preparations to enter the University. These needful arrangements concluded, in the spring of 1768, dressed in knee-breeches, top-boots, a buff waistcoat, and brown velvet cut-away coat, his hair powdered and tied in a cue, and surmounted with a fur hat, he stepped ashore at Williamsburg, from the vessel on which he had taken passage from the banks of the Potomac.

He was now en route for the University of "William and Mary," which had been succeeding under the presidency of the celebrated Doctors Blair and Madison, the latter of whom subsequently became Bishop of Virginia. At this time he was handsome and graceful, and of that delicacy of soul which produces instinctive propriety and gives an easy manner. This facile and graceful manner was improved and finished by his polite education and the familiar intercourse he had enjoyed with the best society of Virginia. His features were oval, his eyes deep blue and animated with sentiment, forehead broad and expansive, nose straight, mouth small, lips thin, chin round, and the whole countenance dignified by a manly aspect. He had nothing of the world's hardened look about him.

After despatching a hasty luncheon at his hotel in Old Dominion Street, for which he had little appetite, his digestive organs having been deranged by a discovery he quickly made as to his toilette, he ordered a tailor to be sent to his room. Thus early had he become conscious that, dressed in the style of a Virginia country gentleman, he was quite behind the age in the commercial capital of the state. The picturesque costume of the Virginian planter of the "olden time," was so decidedly antique and out of fashion in Williamsburg, at least among the juvenile community, that the handsome young stranger was stared out of countenance by the "greedy and devouring" glances cast upon him, not only by the belles who thronged the side-walks, but the public generally. A brief space sufficed to clothe him in the neat not gaudy dress of the beau-monde of that day, and he was afterwards unnoticed in the throng. "Got up" after the prevailing style, he proceeded to deliver the following letter from his father

John Peyton, Esq. to the Honourable Richard Bland.

"Stoney Hill, Virginia,
"March 16th, 1765.

" My dear Bland,

"This letter is entrusted for delivery to my son, John Rowzée, who leaves home in a few days for Williamsburg on his way to the University of 'William and Mary,' where I have supplied him with means to enter himself as a student. Having seen him at Stoney Hill several times, you will have no difficulty in recognizing him now, though he has grown apace, and is much altered in appearance. He is, as you'll see, over six feet high, and, I think, as fine a specimen of the 'Northern neck'[*] as was ever sent from home to acquire, probably, a 'little Latin and less Greek.' Excuse my vanity, but I think you will agree with me that I have reason to be proud of him, when I tell you he has stood at the head of his classes at Dumfries Academy for the last three years, and that he proceeds to the University with the good opinion and kind wishes of Mr. Buchan, his old tutor, and the entire staff of preceptors. Besides this, he handles a cudgel, sits a horse, and rows a boat, equal to any boy in our county. He remains in Williamsburg a few days to procure a supply of books and clothing, and will, probably, need some advice and assistance, so young and inexperienced is he in the ways of the world. He has never been beyond the limits of his native state, except to fish and shoot across the river with our friends in Maryland. I have instructed him to call upon my old friend, Colonel Bland, whose public duties will not, I am persuaded, prevent his giving him any assistance he may require.

"My wife begs me to present her kind compliments to Colonel and Mrs. Bland, and to ask Mrs. B. to fetch her on her return, forty yards of the best black silk for a gown, to which I would be glad you would add ten yards of blue broadcloth for myself. My son will hand you the amount of these purchases in cash. You see, my dear Bland, that we regard you public gentlemen literally in the light of 'public servants.'

"I have nothing to remark upon the subject of your

[*] That portion of Virginia lying between the Rappahannock and Potomac rivers. A high and undulating district, while that south of the Rappahannock is flat. In the northern neck Lord Fairfax had, previous to the American revolution, certain proprietary rights, which yielded him an annual revenue of £15,000.

proceedings in the House of Burgesses, further than that I cordially approve your own course, while I think, as a body, you are disposed to legislate *too much*. I fear a majority of your honourable body have forgotten our popular aphorism, that 'the least governed are the best governed.' I think, therefore, the sooner your deliberations are concluded, the better you'll deserve the thanks of your country. In common with your old friends in Stafford I am anxious to see you back, not, however, altogether upon *public grounds*.

"Mrs. Peyton joins me in most kind regards and remembrances to Mrs. Bland and the young ladies. Believe me,

"Yours truly,
"JOHN PEYTON."

"Colonel Richard Bland, Williamsburg."

Colonel Bland immediately recognised the young gentleman. His memory had been aided by a letter previously received from the young gentleman's father, through the post-office, which had gone by land, and arrived in Williamsburg several days in advance of the vessel which carried him.

Colonel Bland was exceedingly kind and attentive, but rallied his young friend upon the incongruity of his cavalier cue and student's habit. It does not appear, however, that he was successful in causing any abridgement of this venerable relic of the past, as, in a likeness taken fifteen years later, the young gentleman appears with the inevitable pig-tail.

From Williamsburg, he addressed the following letter to his father.

"Old Dominion Hotel, Williamsburg,
"April 10th, 1768.

" My dear father,
"I hasten to inform you of my safe arrival in this city, after a protracted and exceedingly disagreeable voyage. From the time we lost sight of the Potomac until we entered James River, we experienced adverse gales, rain, and all the concomitants that make up what sailors denominate 'dirty weather.' I did not suffer from sea-sickness, but very much from cold and the discomforts inseparable from a sea voyage. I do not know what I should have done without the flannel waistcoats and yarn stockings my dear mother insisted on my taking, and which, during the warm days just preceding my departure, I was disposed to reject as unnecessary, if not effeminating. I found my heavy top-boots of immense service also. With them and an oiled overcoat, the use of which I obtained from a sailor for a few shillings, I braved the worst weather on deck, and found some occupation in watching the shore, in looking out for sails, and gazing upon the ocean 'tempest-tost.'

"I did not, as you directed, proceed immediately on landing to Colonel Bland's, but engaged a tailor to make me a suit of clothes, such as are worn by the gentry here. My own were so behind the fashion, that I was quite an object of curiosity to the people, and took a coach from the vessel to the hotel to prevent annoyance.

"After being renovated by my tailor, I proceeded to Colonel Bland's, and was glad to find him at home, and both astonished and delighted that he recognized me at once from my strong likeness to yourself, for I have always been told that I resembled my mother's family more than yours. He invited me to dinner next day to meet the Honourable Mr. Randolph, Mr. Patrick Henry, Mr. Lewis and a few other public men, all members of the House of Burgesses, and all distinguished for their zeal and public spirit. Of course I accepted his invitation, glad of the opportunity to meet so many of our eminent men with whose names I had long been familiar, and about whom I naturally felt much curiosity The dinner was given at eight o'clock, which I know will be considered preposterous at Stoney Hill, where we take our tea before this hour, and was served up in courses, which I understood from Miss Bland is the French style, and universal in the Williamsburg world of fashion. I will not undertake to give a description of it. Though an excellent repast, I have seen as good, if not better, prepared by my dear mother at old Stoney Hill, only served up in a more homely way, and the food matured with a less infusion of spices, &c.

"Colonel Bland did the honours in an urbane and accomplished manner, but did not shine so much in conversation as Mr. Lewis or Mr. Randolph, nor was he so witty as a Mr. Franklin, of Pennsylvania, who is here on a visit, but on the whole I was proud of him as a representative of old Staffordshire. He is listened to with the greatest respect, and seems to enjoy the confidence and esteem of all. I love the society of men of intellect, extensive information, and honour. I listened to them with delight and sometimes joined in the conversation, (which was free, unreserved, and occasionally animated, almost to the point of discussion), for the purpose of getting explanations upon points which were not always clear to my mind.

"After dinner there was a general party, at which I was presented to many of the reigning beauties, and danced several minuets, but I fear acquitted myself in the midst of such grace, elegance and fashion rather awkwardly. The young ladies were, without exception, splendidly attired, many of them pretty, and in their manners and conversation, I regret to say, much in advance of my sisters and generally of our country girls of the same age—they seem to have quite a fund of information on certain subjects, and are more sprightly and ready in conversation than country belles. One of the most striking of these young ladies was a Miss Harrison, and she was particularly agreeable to me, because of her kind remarks about the country folks, whom she admires more than she does the inhabitants of cities, thinking they are far more sincere and natural. I do not know how it happened, but I chanced to be by her side at the conclusion of the entertainment, and accompanied her home which was in the same street with my hotel. During this short walk, I was with her long enough to make a foolish promise about a visit to her. Nothing is further from my wishes than entering upon a career of fashionable dissipation. I shall avoid rather than court the blandishments of society. In an unguarded moment, however, I made this rash promise. I rather think now, the young lady asked me to call to tell her something about our style of life on the plantations.

"Colonel Bland has done everything in his power to render my visit agreeable, and has placed me under many, very many obligations.

"I shall matriculate at the University to-morrow.

"Give my love to my dear mother, to whom I have written briefly and sent a small package by the 'Flying Dutchman' (the mail coach), and believe me your affectionate son,
"JOHN R. PEYTON."

After delaying a week in Williamsburg, during which he made the acquaintance of many agreeable people, whose friendship he retained through life, he proceeded to "William and Mary" and entered the University, though he did not commence his regular academic studies till the 1st of September following.

He was soon remarked at "William and Mary" by his fellow-students and companions for his superior manliness and gravity of demeanour. He not only passed the usual hours of study over his books, but while others were at play was either engaged with his text or other books. His thirst for knowledge was at this time insatiable. It was during the hours of recreation, that, often in after years he said, he had re-read Rollin's Roman History, 12 vols.—which he regarded as a romance founded upon facts—Herodotus, the History of England, Shakespeare, Gil Blas, and Don Quixote, among a host of other books, useful and entertaining. Notwithstanding these literary studies and occupations, his time was so systematized that he took necessary exercise for the preservation of health, and was trained in all the arts and accomplishments which were regarded as necessary for a gentleman. He was a good fencer and no one sat a horse better.

He early exhibited a strong taste for ethics and metaphysics, and left among his papers several essays or compositions, of unusual interest and ability having reference to these recondite subjects.

In his twentieth year, in 1772, he was graduated as M.A. of the University of William and Mary, and was considered one, if not the most, accomplished scholar ever sent forth from its classic shades. Mr. Macon, (afterwards a distinguished southern jurist,) and himself were regarded as at the head of the university in classical attainments. In mathematics and the natural sciences he was far in advance of all competitors. On entering college, he became a member of a society formed among the students for mutual improvement in the art of public speaking, styled the "Whig Society," and acquired a high reputation among its members for oratorical powers.

Some years subsequent to this period, the Honourable William Dade, a friend and fellow-student at "William and Mary," said of him in a letter addressed to a common friend, " I regard Peyton as in many respects, the most extraordinary speaker I have ever heard. While he is not what you or I would term an orator in the popular sense and acceptation, never addressing himself *ad captandum vulgus*, and seeking to stir the passions of his auditors; he produces an effect on the understanding and heart of those he addresses, which no oratory could surpass. His logic is clear and irresistible, his ideas quick and just, his manner and style fascinating to such an extent that you can scarcely listen without being carried away."

These opinions of competent judges among his contemporaries are introduced, lest it may be supposed that natural partiality and affection have betrayed the writer into undistinguished praise, which he seeks to avoid as being weak, as it is unjust, reflecting neither credit upon the encomiast nor the person commended. It is not pretended that the young gentleman was a prodigy, combining the character of the poet, the orator and hero—providence is very rarely so lavish of its gifts to one man. But that his moral and intellectual qualities were of a very high order is incontestible. Method requires, that, in this brief sketch, the character of the youthful author of the mass of letters herein incorporated and made part of this narrative, should be explained at the outset.

The heart warms towards the young when they are seen starting joyfully forth on the journey of life; for, in the words of a quaint Scotch writer, " It is a troublous water, the water of life; and it has often given me a sore heart to see the young things launched upon it like bairns' boats, sailing hither and thither in an unpurposelike manner, having no thought of who it is that sends both the soft wind and the storm; and, if they have need of various instruments and a right pilot man to guide ships over that constant uncertainty, the sea, I think not but there is far greater need of all manner of helps to pass safely through that greater uncertainty—life."

CHAPTER III.

HE VISITS NEW YORK.—IS SHIPWRECKED ON THE RETURN VOYAGE.—HIS ACCOUNT OF THE AFFAIR.—HE COMMENCES THE STUDY OF MILITARY ENGINEERING AND THE ART OF WAR UNDER COLONEL DE BLOIS IN RICHMOND.

AFTER the close of his university career, as mentioned in the previous chapter, he returned to the home of his boyhood, from which he had gone forth eight years before, and which he had since visited only during the usual school and college vacations. One may imagine the affectionate pride with which he was welcomed back by his family and friends, upon whom he had reflected so much credit.

The following letter which he addressed to one of his intimate collegiate friends, Mr. Williams, supplies some interesting information of himself at this period, and carries forward the narrative.

"Stoney Hill, Virginia, September 20th, 1772.

" Dear Williams,
"After our adieux in Philadelphia, I met Gaston and Ingersol,* who accompanied me to New York, according to previous arrangements, where, after two days, we left Ingersol discussing democracy with his radical friends. Taking the 'Blue Belle' for Alexandria, Gaston and I arrived there, after a disagreeable and dangerous voyage. We were overtaken by a storm off the northern capes of

* Two of his fellow students.

Virginia, and but for a painful accident, resulting in the destruction of a boat, and the death of seven of her freight of human beings, should have been lost; in other words, their loss was our gain. To the chapter of accidents alone, are you indebted for this letter.

"On the first day of the storm the sky was obscured by immense masses of clouds, surcharged with inflammable matter; and in the evening the rain fell in torrents, the firmament darkened apace, sudden night came on, and the horrors of extreme darkness were rendered still more horrible by the peals of thunder which rent the air, and the frequent flashes of lightning, which served only to show us the terrors of our situation, and leave us in greater darkness.

"On the next morning, the gale increased to a hurricane, and the sea ran mountain high. Our rigging was so strained with the work, and the wind blew so persistently towards the coast, that the captain and officers became seriously alarmed lest we should not be able to weather the coast. During the morning, many of the sails flew into ribbons, and some of the rigging was carried away—soon every remaining sail in the vessel was gone, and the whole ship presented a dreadful and mortifying spectacle. Fear and despondency reduced the crew to helplessness. The captain raved liked a madman, while many of the men were cast upon their knees, clapping their hands, and praying with all the extravagance of horror painted in their faces. The only undismayed persons were two ladies and a party of half-drunken ruffians, who had taken possession of the deck, and were preparing to launch a boat. Both Gaston and myself sought to bring the captain back to reason, and to a sense of what he owed to his duty as a commander, and to his dignity as a man; we exhorted him to encourage the sailors by his example, and sought to reassure him by declaring that though the vessel might be lost, the passengers could be saved. That though the storm was terrific, we had seen the sea more furious. Our exertions had the happiest effect, and in a short time a number of the crew were working at the pumps and throwing overboard our freight. At mid-day the weather cleared up a little, and the wind and the sea seemed to have abated. As the weather grew better, and the sea less furious, the senses of the people returned, and the general stupification began to decrease. The captain now determined to make an effort to land the passengers in small boats on a point of land two miles distant. The first boat was made ready, in which he directed, among others, Gaston, myself, and three ladies to proceed, if possible, ashore. We went below at this time to secure our money and a few valuables, principally jewels, intended as presents to our sisters, expecting, of course, to lose our luggage. Remounting to the deck, we found the boat launched, but in custody of a party of ruffians —who had taken possession of the deck, and now defied the captain's authority. Both Gaston and myself expressed our willingness to the captain to aid in an attempt to rescue the boat before they could shove off, but Captain Villiers declined making the effort, as from the size of their party, and the confusion resulting from the storm, the issue of such a step was doubtful. He preferred, indeed, to allow them to leave the ship, thinking he could save us in the remaining boat. One by one the mutineers hurried into the boat, as well as they could, in the midst of the storm, leaving the ladies on deck. All being aboard, they pushed off and endeavoured to make the shore. We now set to work to launch a second craft. While thus occupied, shrieks were heard proceeding from the water, and it was observed with horror that the boat had swamped, and the men were struggling in the angry waters. At the time, the wind was driving us ahead with frightful rapidity, and there was little prospect that we could be of service to the unfortunate creatures; but humanity triumphed over every other consideration, and Captain Villiers, notwithstanding their infamous conduct, and his own eminent danger, used his best efforts to aid them, by casting overboard spars, deal boards and other articles, hoping that some at least might save themselves. Through these humane exertions of our amiable, but weak commander, five of them were rescued, having been thrown ashore during the night, while seven perished.

"At a favourable moment the second boat was sent adrift with the ladies, Gaston, myself, and the crew, Villiers being in command. We had scarcely abandoned the ship before she struck the ground. Next morning we could see nothing of her—she had disappeared, and had evidently broken up, as the main-mast was already washed ashore. A few hours later, we safely made the shore, and on the next day arrived in Norfolk, from which point we crossed to Gloucester county, and thence reached home. Such in brief is the account of our wreck, which I might exhaust pages in describing, without giving you an adequate idea of its horrors.

"Occurrences such as that I have described, of the men seizing the boat, and, disregarding the claims of the weak and defenceless—I mean, of the ladies—and afterwards reaping the reward of their cruel and cowardly conduct, may be thought by some too trivial to be mentioned; but I trust that I shall ever be enabled to look upon the deliverance of these poor ladies, myself and friend, from the danger of entering the first boat, as of every other kind of danger, as the secret, but certain effects of that over-ruling Providence, to whose care I thankfully acknowledge myself indebted for my present safety. At sea, our immediate dependence on the Almighty strikes us in a solemn manner. Happy is he who knows Him as a friend and father, and can place his confidence in Him whilst on that dreadful element!"   *   *   *   *   *

"Gaston came with me and remained a week, then leaving for Alexandria, where he has many friends and acquaintances. He is a Roman Catholic in faith, and my sister, Lucy, told him yesterday she thought he must be going to Alexandria, where there is a Catholic church, to make confession. While he was staying with me, we made two interesting visits ; one to the Pembrokes, in Maryland, where there are some pretty young ladies, to whom I think there is a greater probability of his confessing than to any of the priesthood. The other was to Richmond, to make arrangements for studying military engineering under Colonel de Blois, formerly a distinguished officer in the French service, but now living in exile at Richmond. But more upon this subject at another time."

* * * * *

As intimated in this letter, he shortly afterwards proceeded to Richmond, and entered zealously upon his professional studies. While thus occupied, he received the following letter from his father, which called him home, and gave a new direction to his plans, and a totally different result to his life than any that could, at this period, have been reasonably anticipated.

"Stoney Hill, May 6th, 1773.

"I hasten to advise my dear John, that I have made arrangements with Mr., commonly called, Captain John Skinner, of the brig 'Frolic,' lying at Alexandria, to ship my crop of tobacco to the West Indies. Captain Skinner has also been informed that you are to accompany him on this voyage, to execute numerous commissions for and on my behalf. I shall confide the sale of my tobacco and other articles I purpose shipping, to my agents in Jamaica, as also the task of purchasing such supplies as I require on my plantation, with a list of which they will be duly furnished. It is upon different matters altogether that I wish you to proceed to the West Indies. These I shall explain when you reach home. My object in writing this hurried note is to say that I wish you to return at the earliest possible moment. You will immediately, therefore, upon the receipt of this writing, make your arrangements to quit Richmond, and after taking your leave of such kind friends as you may desire to bid adieu, repair hither with the utmost diligence.

"I regret exceedingly the interruption it will occasion in your studies, but I think you will agree with me in the propriety and advantages of the trip, when I shall have explained its nature. You must have already perceived, that the well-being of my children is my first, I might, perhaps, without trespassing much upon truth, say, my only object in life; that to the care of their education, and the cultivation of their minds and hearts I exclusively devote my time and my thoughts; and that to ensure their future happiness, I would sacrifice everything I have a right to dispose of, and risk even life itself. I trust you are not unmindful of the obligations, the important duty it enforces on you, and that your only emulation will be how most abundantly to reward my labours, which, in the end, will be to reward yourself.

"Pray obtain from Mr. Dennison a copy of the deed for the land purchased of him, and a box of books and papers which I left with Mr. John Randolph. Fetch these in your 'trap.' The box will not be too bulky to be strapped behind your chaise. Call upon Henry Watson, in Fredericksburg, and collect £175 he owes me for turpentine. I send you herein his 'I O U.' You may find the money convenient in making your preparations for the journey.

"Captain Skinner desires me to say that it is necessary you should be in Alexandria against the 16th, as he designs, wind and weather permitting, to set sail on that day.

"Give yourself no concern about procuring an outfit for the voyage, in Richmond. You can purchase every requisite article, *tout-à-fait,* in Alexandria. Your mother joins me in much love to our dear son, and I am, though in great haste, "Your affectionate father,
"JOHN PEYTON."

"John Rowzée Peyton, Esq. Church Hill, Richmond."

CHAPTER IV.

HE LEAVES RICHMOND AND RETURNS TO STONEY HILL.—SAILS FOR THE WEST INDIES.—HIS ACCOUNT OF THE VOYAGE.—SICKNESS ON BOARD THE VESSEL. —SCARCITY OF WATER.—STORM OFF THE NORTH CAROLINA COAST.—SIGHT THE FRENCH KEYS.—LANDS AT TICHFIELD AND DINES WITH THE PRESIDENT.

WITHOUT a moment's hesitation, he proceeded, immediately upon the receipt of the letter which concludes the last preceding chapter, to make his preparations to leave Richmond. He saw, not without pain, his plans of study thus frustrated at a most interesting period—he hoped it would be only for a brief season—but such were his ideas of duty, and such his filial piety and the natural warmth of his affection for his parents, there was no sacrifice he was unwilling to make in their behalf.

Arrived at Stoney Hill, he entered energetically upon his preparations for the journey, and, these completed, proceeded to Alexandria and went aboard the "Frolic," May the 20th, 1773. It appears, from the following letter addressed to his father, and dated upon that vessel, nine days subsequently (May 29th, 1773), when at sea, that the brig was detained three days longer at Alexandria than he anticipated.

"We were unable to sail before the 23rd, having been

unexpectedly, and I may add unaccountably, delayed in getting a portion of our cargo aboard. The task, however, was completed on that day, and we dropped down the river, and came to opposite the mouth of the Rappahannock. Here, to our infinite annoyance, we tailed on the ground, and quietly settled in the mud, against the rising of the next tide. This misadventure was, according to the assertions of the pilot, unavoidable. There was much doubt, however, in which I participated, whether he had diligently and faithfully discharged his duty. During the night the wind shifted to the west, and we warped into the channel, and were out of danger, and in a fair way to sail, without any thanks to the pilot, when sufficiently light. Being now in the current, it was necessary to drop an anchor. The bedge anchor was carried out twice, but, the ground being soft, it came home both times. Dropping down the river a half mile with the current, our anchor caught and held in the oyster shoals. Our pilot was now apparently on the other extreme, and suffering from an excess of caution. He proceeded slowly, seemed averse to anything like speed, and altogether impressed me as being a worthless fellow, as belonging, indeed, to that numerous class of inefficients so happily characterized as the 'easy-going, good for nothing.'

"The morning of the 26th was bright and pleasant, with an easy gale. We set sail about sunrise, and made rapid headway, assisted by the current. The weather continued mild and agreeable, and the wind favourable throughout the day. About 3 P.M. we passed out of the river into the broad and magnificent Chesapeake Bay, and sighted lights from fishermen's huts off the northern capes at three o'clock in the morning. Leaving the first buoy at the entrance into the Sound on our port side, and hauling up all we could to weather the next, we left it on the starboard quarter. The wind freshened considerably during the night, and shifting to an adverse quarter, we were detained off the Virginia Capes till the 28th. On the forenoon of this day, the wind becoming favourable, we parted with our pilot, and made sail for Tichfield, Jamaica. The captain proposed going the windward passage, and for this reason to make the French Keys. The favourable weather of the 28th continued to the 30th, when, just before day, while off Cape Hatteras, it blew half a gale. Everything was rolled and tossed about the deck in wild disorder. Most negligently, nothing had hitherto been secured against such an accident. Order scarcely yet reigned in our craft, and no precautions were taken against the likeliest contingencies During the 'blow' I was sea-sick—very, but soon recovered when the winds abated. On the 31st we hailed a schooner from Salem, Massachusetts, whence she had been forty days, having put into the Bermudas. She was freighted with rum, and bound for Pimlico River, to load with tar for London. The wind continuing to blow hard on the 1st of June, we were driven from our course. Captain Skinner was ill to-day with fever and ague. We found the chief mate an ignorant and idle fellow. I feared with bad weather and worse management, disabled and inferior officers, we were not likely to have a 'good time generally' in the 'Frolic.' I consoled myself, however, with *nous verrons*, and certainly the result has been more satisfactory than I anticipated.

"On the 2nd of June we had reached the 29th degree of latitude, the weather continuing moderate. In order to elevate the spirits of the crew, the captain, who had shaken off his ague, ordered a sheep and pig to be divided among them, and a half dozen bottles of rum to be sent to the mess. Several of the men were now ill with dysentery and fever. Proper care was not taken to keep the vessel clean, and our water was sadly squandered. I hoped we should not suffer for the want of it before the voyage was over. For seven days succeeding the 2nd, nothing special occurred, the winds were prosperous and the skies bright and serene. On the 9th of June we had reached the 27th degree of latitude, but the ship was badly steered, and we were much out of our course. Such at least was the reported result of this day's observations. Captain Skinner informed me that he had some thought of making the Cape, east of Hispaniola. Of course I was too ignorant of navigation to be able to advise him how to sail his vessel most advantageously. The weather was now beginning to be very much warmer, and the captain ordered the brig to be cleansed and purified. It thus became more comfortable. This course, indeed, alone prevented some distemper from being bred amongst the men. Having taken a severe cold, and not knowing what else to do, I bled myself this day, understanding from an old sailor, accustomed to the Indies, that it is esteemed conducive to the health under the tropics. While engaged in the operation, I could not help having ludicrous ideas recurring to memory of our friend Dr. Sangrado. The fine weather at this period and better health of the crew, with the prospect of a short and prosperous voyage, gave an air of cheerfulness to all on board. Several also of those who had been confined with fever, reappeared upon deck. Our stock of provisions was good and proved more than ample for our wants, but we were throughout sadly in want of good liquors. Our beer spoiled, and our cider proved indifferent. Rum and whiskey seem to be too fiery for the climate, which day by day, waxed hotter and hotter. I used them but gingerly myself, thinking it rather unphilosophic while reducing the fever of the system by blood letting, to keep up the fires with inferior rum.

"During the twenty-four hours, preceding the 12th of June, the weather was deliciously bright and genial. The captain availed himself of this excellent opportunity to take an account of the provisions and water already expended. Disagreeably enough it proved to be half our stock. This result confirmed my views, as to the extravagant and wasteful use we had been making of it. And I conjectured that we should be cut off of our supply when we most needed it: The warm weather greatly increased our thirst and the necessity for a full supply of water. To husband what remained, I suggested to the captain that no one should take water from the barrels except in presence of an officer, and then be required to suck it through a reed. No one could thereby take more than he could drink, and if it were only so used, our supply I thought would be ample. He agreed to this, and a sentry was placed over the cask on deck. While on deck that day, I saw a shoal of porpoise disporting themselves in the water, and in the air many of the feathered tribe peculiar to these latitudes. The wind sprung up a fine easy gale this forenoon, and we got up our top gallant masts and yards. On the 13th of June, we made land, which we supposed was the French Keys, distance about six leagues. At seven o'clock we stood off under our foresail and reefed topsails, and during the day arrived off Acklin Island and steered directly for Great Magna, intending to pass between it and the Island of Cuba. In passing we obtained a very good view. On the coast and to the east the land is low, but rises towards the interior. In the west, the land rises higher than elsewhere, and on the coast there are some steep rugged cliffs.

"The moderation and serenity of the atmosphere since our arrival in the West Indies has excited general remark. The heat has not been oppressive, from the frequency of showers of rain, and the prevalence of breezes. Passing between Cuba and Hispaniola, we sighted the northern shores of Jamaica on the 17th of June. The bold and rugged features of the coast struck us with delight. During the forenoon the captain hauled up and stood to the windward, expecting a pilot, though at so great a distance. He was not satisfied that we were before Tichfield. though from the mast-head I saw buildings and smoke from the land, as well as a boat with sails lying in front of what I took to be the harbour. We were still three leagues distant, and the captain thought the harbour could not be seen at a greater distance than one league ahead. He stood in to shore however, and after an hour's sailing, was himself convinced that we were opposite the town, but the sea running high he would not stand in for it, until a pilot came aboard. I determined, however, to go ashore in the yawl, with two seamen whom the captain ordered to accompany me, though we were still nearly two leagues distant. Notwithstanding the high sea we arrived safely. I found the experience I had acquired in boating on the Potomac, of no little value on this occasion. As we entered the harbour we found a boat going off to the brig with a pilot. This boat had attempted to reach us before, but was forced to put back by the heavy sea. I waited upon the President and authorities, who treated me with great courtesy, and promised us any and every assistance we might require. The President was kind enough to insist upon my dining with him the next day.

"From his residence I proceeded to call upon your correspondents, Messrs. Howell, Williams, and Holton, and explained to them the nature of my visit, delivering to them your letters. While thus occupied, the 'Frolic' stood in to shore, and in less than two hours after I had established myself at the inn, was at anchor in the harbour.

"A word as to the harbour and town will not be misplaced at this point. On either side of the town there are two prominent rocks or points of land, one to the eastward, and the other opposite on the extremity of Navy Island. Between these two points and commanding them both lies the fort, on what is called the northern isthmus. It effectually guards the entrance and covers the town of Tichfield, which lies to the rear. There are now in port a Newcastle brig, with coals which have been sold at Kingston, where the brig takes in a return cargo of rum and sugar for London. Also four other vessels—one loading with mahogany and lignum vitæ for New England, and the others with sugar and ginger for Liverpool. You will conclude from this that Tichfield is a place of thriving business, especially when I inform you that fewer vessels than usual are now in port. The town is well situated on rising ground. The lots are generally 70 feet front by 150 feet in depth and are valued at from £200 to £300 according to situation. The buildings are almost without exception of wood, are built without taste or ornament, are generally dilapidated and many of them unoccupied. I was informed in explanation of this condition of affairs that since the conclusion of the peace with the wild negroes inhabiting the mountainous districts of the interior, many families, who had been driven to the town for safety during the continuance of hostilities, had returned to the country to engage again in agriculture.

"There is something quaint and foreign in every thing which meets the eye in this portion of His Majesty's widely extended dominions. This alone invests Jamaica with peculiar interest to myself. Civilization, or what we call by that ambitious name, is making such strides that I suppose we shall soon be able to travel through every land without observing anything in the edifices, the people, their dress, manners, or customs, to distinguish one nation from another. The grey or bright sky, the cold or warm atmosphere, the stunted or luxuriant vegetation will alone indicate change of place. Alas! that this seems inevitable; that the picturesque costumes, the local habits and customs of the past, which lent a kind of changeful grace to every fresh town or province of a new country, awakening in the traveller poetic thoughts and bright fancies, should disappear before the stern touch of our utilitarian philosophy! Here in Jamaica every thing still bears the impress of foreign upon it, and it elates and gladdens my heart.

"The day following I dined with the President according to invitation, and met with much kindness and civility. The dinner was substantial and good. We had boiled beef and greens, a fine turkey and saddle of excellent mutton, a goose with 'papau' sauce, which much resembles, but is superior to, apple sauce, a boiled pudding and a baked pumpkin. For drink we had French and Madeira wines, strong beer and punch made with fresh fruit, with which the island abounds. The company consisted of sixteen persons, besides the President and his wife, most of whom were officers from the fort, and strangers of distinction in the town. The entertainment passed off pleasantly, though several of the guests followed their legs under the President's mahogany before the punch was exhausted. The guests called upon me next day, without exception, and none complained of headache, which is no small compliment to the excellence of the wines in Jamaica.

"You will observe that I am concluding upon dry land this letter which I commenced while at sea. I need scarcely add that I am doing so under circumstances more comfortable than those surrounding me when off Cape Hatteras, so unenviably notorious for its storms. As it is to be confided to a Mr. Green, who leaves on the 'Venus' to-night, bound for Charleston, S.C., where he has promised me to drop it in the post, I must needs be brief, and am somewhat hurried. So far I can communicate nothing more definite upon matters of business than that your merchants and agents inform me that there will be fair sale for your tobacco, which will be re-shipped to England, and no difficulty in filling your orders for purchases. I have transferred along with your letters the list you gave me to Messrs. Howell and Williams, and as they understand such matters better than myself, leave it to them to be executed. Upon other interesting matters I will write at another time, and without delay. To-morrow I leave on a tour of the principal objects of interest in the eastern end of the island, and upon my return within a fortnight will report the progress your agents have made. There is no probability that we will be able to set sail on our return before the 15th of August, as the brig requires repairs."

CHAPTER V.

SOME ACCOUNT OF SCENERY AND NATURAL PRODUCTIONS OF JAMAICA.—THE SLAVES.—A SUGAR PLANTATION.—BAD HUSBANDRY.—A NEGRO DEVICE FOR TAKING FISH.—FRUITS AND FLOWERS.—MOUNTAIN ROADS.—CAPTAIN PELHAM, R.E.—SPANISH TOWN.—ENTERTAINMENT BY THE GOVERNOR.—UNEXPECTED MEETING WITH A PARTY OF VIRGINIANS.—SOCIETY IN JAMAICA.

THE particular object of his visit to Jamaica nowhere appears in this correspondence. Whatever it may have been, it does not seem to have made serious demands upon his time and energies. Shortly after the date of the foregoing letter, giving an account of his outward journey, he wrote the one next succeeding, dated "Spanish Town, Jamaica, June 28th, 1773," from which it is seen that his visit to Tichfield was as brief as pleasant.

"Feeling much anxiety to visit some of the objects of interest in the island during my sojourn, especially as my presence in Tichfield was not required in connection with your affairs, I left ten days ago for Spanish Town. Of this place, which is the seat of government, I shall have more to say anon. Captain Pelham accompanies me, and will most probably continue my *compagnon du voyage* throughout. For making the journey we procured three inferior saddle horses in Tichfield, and a guide, agreeing to pay for all £17 6s. to and from Spanish Town. If the guide and horses were detained, it was further agreed we should pay for additional delay in like proportion. The charge is exorbitant; but—there is always a 'but' in everything—no better arrangement was possible, and neither Captain Pelham nor myself were disposed to abandon the project of seeing a considerable part of the island from ill-advised considerations of economy. After travelling five miles over a rocky and uneven road, running through a fertile country covered with a luxuriant vegetation, where many delicious fruits were growing spontaneously, we reached the River Grande. At this point we bid adieu to Mr. Roberts and Major Ogilvy, who accompanied us to this point merely for the pleasure of a ride.

"On either side of the road there were cultivated crops of cotton, sugar, indigo, corn and ginger; but the husbandry was careless and the enclosures neglected. We forded the river on horseback, the water reaching to our saddle skirts. The current is swift, and the bottom smooth and pebbly. Where the stream spreads out and becomes shallow, stones are thrown out upon either side in the water, forming a narrow 'chute,' at the mouth of which a trap of wicker work is 'set' for the purpose of taking fish This is a negro contrivance, and answers a good purpose. On the south side of the river the hills are high and steep, but the vallies between them green and fertile. A stream gurgles through every valley, or falls in spray from every hill side. Indeed it is one of the most admirably and conveniently watered countries imaginable. Having its source in the mountains the water can be readily and inexpensively used for purposes of irrigation. Passing a small stream called Spanish river, and some lagoons of salt water, only separated from the sea by a narrow strip of beach, through which the sea water percolates, we arrived at Bluff Bay, where there are a few dwellings and some sugar works. Here we remained the night, in the house of a planter, Mr. Johnson, to whom we were recommended. He treated us with much civility, and entertained us in sumptuous style. Mr. Johnson is a large land and slave owner, having between 70 and 100 working or field hands. His sugar works are extensive, and the plantation well supplied with horses, oxen and farming implements of every description. The morning following our arrival we rode over his estate, and were much gratified. We saw twenty yoke of oxen ploughing, and a party of fifty slaves labouring in one field. The land is securely enclosed, well cultivated, and in high tilth and condition. Though Mr. Johnson relies principally for income upon sugar, he grows small quantities of cotton, coffee and rice. His slaves were well, though lightly clad, comfortably lodged, and apparently contented and happy.

"Bidding this hospitable planter adieu about noon, we proceeded upon our journey. Turning from the sea-board, we pursued a deep valley, through which water was trickling from every rock, leading to the mountains. The ascent of these was steep and difficult, the road being infamous. To prevent our saddles sliding over the horses' tails, we had one of the girths carried around their breasts. On either side of us, above and below, there was much grand and beautiful scenery. Many of the trees are of prodigious size, and of the most valuable species of timber, such as mahogany, teak and cedar. One of the indigenous fruits is the banana, which is of a peculiarly delicate flavour. We also saw plantains, yams, eddoes, cassavi, and sweet potatoes. I must not forget to mention that one of their trees most prized is the log-wood, which seems to have come largely into use in this town as a colouring matter for wines. Some of the wines we have sipped seem, indeed, to be composed of one half logwood and the other catsup. The Blue Mountains we crossed, extend from one extremity of the island to the other, rising in some parts nearly 8,500 feet above the level of the sea. Unlike Virginian mountains they are generally conical in shape, the three highest being respectively 7,500, 7,600 and 8,200 feet high. The ravines between these lofty peaks are commonly denominated, for what reason I am unadvised, 'cock-pits.' There are many varieties of soil, and all are fertile. In the high mountains the productions differ from those in the vallies. Only in the vallies and plains are cotton, pimento and coffee cultivated. In the loftier regions, crops are grown which require less warmth and sunshine.

"One night we stopped at Oakenwold, a very neat and pretty timber house, belonging to a Mr. Pryor. It stands in a wide valley, where there are extensive sugar works. The prospect of the country from the mountains to the south, over the broad and fertile plain which lies between them and the sea, is exceedingly beautiful. It is dotted over with towns and villages, country seats, farm buildings, sugar works and negro huts. Approaching the town of Kingston we met a multitude of negroes, principally women, returning from the place where they had gone to sell their garden produce and fetch back their purchases. In their white gowns, coloured turbans, with baskets of golden fruit upon their heads, they formed picturesque groups strongly suggestive of the Oriental. Turning from the road leading directly to Kingston we followed another which conducted us to Spanish Town. Upon our arrival the streets were filled with a curious crowd of people of many colours. This piebald collection was attracted by the assizes, which are held quarterly by the Chief Justice and two associate justices These insular judges are not esteemed learned in the law, but their judgments at which they arrive by a common sense process of reasoning, are less frequently reversed than those of the higher court, which is presided over by a professional lawyer. Thus it seems that in the Jamaica courts 'a little learning' has ceased to be 'a dangerous thing.'

"We were much fatigued by our journey; the latter part of the time finding it difficult to spur on the horses, who were much jaded and very lame. The custom of shoeing horses has not found its way to this island, and ours had their hoofs so broken and worn away that they could scarcely shuffle along after the first day.

"After establishing ourselves in the principal inn, we proceeded to saunter through the town. It was built by the Spaniards, and hence its name. The houses are low, and without grace or beauty. Built in every style of architecture, notwithstanding their inferiority, the appearance of the whole is quaint and picturesque.

"The Governor is spending the summer three miles in the country, but is daily for two hours in his town office. Here we called upon His Excellency, and were received with great civility. He seemed much interested in Virginia, and made many inquiries about our habits and customs, climate, soil and productions. He invited us to dinner next day, and hearing that we were travelling on horseback, proposed to send his chariot to fetch us. Thanking him warmly, we declined putting him to such trouble. He now insisted with so much pertinacity, that we could but let him have his own way. He gave us a handsome and substantial dinner, at which his wife presided, and which was graced by the presence of his two daughters. We were charmed with their pleasant manners and sprightly conversation. Both the Madeira and the French wines were of excellent quality and fine flavour. The Madeira, however, does not ripen so well in this as in our Virginian climate. I know you will smile at my undertaking to have opinions of *my own* upon the subject of wines, that wine against which you have inveighed so strongly, as certain in the end to ' bite like a serpent and sting like an adder.' My opinion may be of very little value to others, but is of importance, as you'll allow, to myself; so much so, that I may say with Solomon ' whosoever is deceived thereby is not wise.' In regard to what I eat and drink, I praise that which pleases me. *Chacun à son goût.* I hope I may say this much without the fear of your classing me among ' wine-bibbers ; among riotous eaters of flesh.'

"The day following this entertainment, Captain Pelham and myself hired a chariot and four, (for which we paid two pistoles) and invited the Governor's lady and daughters to drive. They were pleased to accept, and we drove to the port, a distance of six miles. Returning, we proceeded to the Governor's town house, situated on the Parade, an unpretending looking building on the exterior, but containing many good and well furnished apartments within. After taking a glass of wine and looking at his extensive variety of flowers, we proceeded to the Course. Here were assembled the *élite* or 'quality,' as the negroes call the fashionables, riding, driving, or promenading for the benefit of air and exercise.

"Spanish Town was now rife with a rumour that two Virginians had arrived, and were the guests of His Excellency, that they were of distinguished birth and enormous wealth, and that they were unmarried, and if not in quest of, had no particular objection to taking wives. The latter fact created intense excitement among managing mammas, looking after eligible connections for their daughters. During our drive all eyes were turned upon us, and though neither Pelham nor myself are particularly sensitive, we were somewhat disconcerted. His Excellency's daughters were quite facetious over the sensation we had so innocently created, and declared that we should not leave town without having a better opportunity of seeing those who took so much interest in us. They therefore gave us invitations to an evening entertainment to take place two days later. Though our time was running short we could not refuse this kind and polite invitation, and we accordingly made our preparations to attend. The item you will discover in my list of expenses of £30 paid for a new suit of clothes will require no further explanation. It illustrates the immediate connection between business and pleasure.

The Governor's ball, for it turned out to be such, though prepared hurriedly and on short notice, was gay and brilliant. All the most distinguished for rank, wealth, and station in this part of the island to the number of 150 were present. There was dancing for the young and cards for the old—supper and wine for all. The supper was such as only Jamaica can supply—such a profusion and variety of delicious fruits I never saw.

"You may imagine my surprise on finding one of the most distinguished beauties and accomplished ladies at this entertainment, Miss Annie Howe of the Occoquan in Virginia. She is the daughter of Howson Howe, Esq., of Belleville, whose name I have often heard and with which you must be familiar. Miss Howe, who has been in delicate health, came here last autumn, accompanied by her mother, and though she has entirely recovered, will remain the next winter, in order to consolidate her strength. Mrs. Howe informs me that her husband, who is now in London, having sailed thence from Kingston, will return early in November. The family will pass the winter between Spanish Town and Kingston, and sail for Virginia the following May. I have formed a pleasant acquaintance with them, and we have had many interesting conversations concerning our friends and affairs in Virginia. Mrs. Howe has twice been in your company without, however, making your acquaintance—once at Mr. R. Goods, in Chesterfield, and again at Tuckahoe, the seat of Mr. Mann Randolph. Miss Howe is most accomplished, amiable, and intelligent, possessing, so far as I can judge, every good quality in an eminent degree. Young, wise, fair, she is the acknowledged belle of Spanish Town, and is yet so unaffected by the admiration she creates, so thoroughly good tempered, so affable and agreeable, that she has excited not the slightest enmity or jealousy among her less gifted female friends. Though the brightest ornament of this society, beloved and admired by all, she does not surrender herself altogether to the blandishments of fashionable life. Frequently, when her companions are pleasure seeking, she from choice remains at home, to put the finishing touch to a drawing or piece of embroidery. But the honest pride I feel in this fair representative of our colony will be mistaken for another sentiment, if I allow myself to dwell longer upon this interesting subject.

"The society of Spanish Town, though small is excellent. The pleasure of a residence here is considerably marred however by the arbitrary lines of distinction which are drawn between the different classes. The old families, who alone belong to what are called the *pur sang*, are the descendants of the first colonists, and many of these trace their descent from the Norman invaders of England; others penetrating beyond that period known as 'time whereof the memory of man runneth not to the contrary,' produce their genealogies and pedigrees, bringing down their descent through the Scandinavians from the Asiatics. Those who indulge in this weak ambition affect sovereign contempt for the middle classes, for all, indeed, who have risen to dignities through trade, or 'dirt,' as they express it, more forcibly than elegantly; and hence the community, which should be united and harmonious, for the common happiness of all, is rent in factions and embittered by feuds. It really seems to me, much as I have heard in Virginia upon this subject of old families, that of all vanity it is the most extravagant; for if antiquity be the object, all are equally high, since all must have originated from the same stock. If the pride be to belong to a particular family who were distinguished for valour or virtue, it cannot apply to a whole community. To such an extent is this upstart feeling carried in Jamaica, that the favourite study is heraldry and genealogy. Many who have risen to wealth by cultivating coffee and distilling rum, have immediately turned their backs upon those interesting and useful articles, and employed themselves in manufacturing a pedigree. The ablest members of the College of Heralds in London, however, have been uniformly unable to send these forth, except with wanting links, bars sinister and great gaps, rents and fissures, which remind one of a book with pages here and there torn from it. Still they pride themselves on this 'open work' style of genealogy: have these fancy documents recorded with their arms, newly invented, and at the end of fifty years assume what they suppose to be the airs of patricians. While genuine aristocrats hold them in contempt, the middle classes treat with the bitterest ridicule their spurious superiority."

CHAPTER VI.

HE VISITS CARTHAGENA.—CITY AND BAY.—CHURCHES.—POPULAR IGNORANCE AND SUPERSTITION.—THE SIEGE OF 1741.—DEATH OF HIS UNCLE.—A NORTH CAROLINIAN.—RETURNS TO JAMAICA.—ANNIE HOWE, THE BRIGHT PARTICULAR STAR OF SPANISH TOWN.—BRIEF ACCOUNT OF JAMAICA CONCEIVED IN THE RIGHT SPIRIT.

NOTWITHSTANDING the business engagements which carried him to Jamaica, as we must infer from his father's letter, addressed to him in Richmond; the blandishments of society in Spanish Town; and last though not least, the charms of his fair countrywoman, Annie Howe; we find from the succeeding letter that he tore himself from the island, to drop a tear upon the grave of a gallant and distinguished relative. This uncle left Virginia more than thirty years anterior to this date, to take part in the English expedition against Carthagena in 1741, and perished in that abortive enterprise. He gives so full an account of this excursion, that his next letter, dated at Carthagena, July, 1773, requires no further introduction, but is left to tell its own story.

"My principal object in visiting this particular place, as you may readily imagine, was to look upon the scene of my uncle Robert's exploits in 1741, and stand by his honoured tomb. Never can I forget the impression made upon my imagination, while yet a child, by the history of his adventures, so often related by my dear mother and yourself.

"Setting sail from Kingston with a light land breeze, we proceeded a short distance to sea, when the wind veered and was directly in 'our teeth.' For the next three days we continued much in the same manner, but soon more favourable weather prevailing, we made the harbour of Carthagena. The appearance of this fortified place from the water, is, in a scenic point of view, attractive, but the fortifications on all sides convey the most disagreeable sensations, reminding one of war—the first misery of mankind.

"Though trained, and for some time past accustomed to military habits, as Colonel de Blois would say, the 'dreadful note of preparation' in these strong and numerous fortifications was most unpleasing. The feelings of man and citizen claim a paramount right to my heart. What do all these guns and fortresses mean, but the disposition of man to violate the rights of his fellow-creatures, and the tyrannic abuse of power?

"The city is situated upon a low piece of marsh land, close upon the sea-side. It is surrounded by canals, natural and artificial. The climate is hot, and the lakes and salt marshes give forth a deadly malaria, during the autumn causing great mortality among strangers. The natives, however, seem to enjoy an exemption from disease. Though much oppressed at times by the heat, my health and strength are unaffected. I attribute this to the even tenor of my life, to regular exercise, and my free use of the cold bath, which seems also to have its influence upon the mind, or as the inimitable poet Thomson expresses it,

"'—— from the body's purity, the mind
Receives a secret sympathetic aid.'

"I have had sufficient experience of the effect of climate and change of season upon the constitution, especially with reference to those whose frames are delicate and whose sensibility is acute, to totally dissent from the remarks of Mr. Samuel Johnson, that 'distinction of season is produced only by imagination, operating on luxury.' This giant of the pen never uttered, so far as my experience and observations extend, a greater fallacy, more sententiously, when he continues 'To temperance every day is bright, and every hour is propitious to diligence. He that shall resolutely excite his faculties, or exert his virtues, will soon make himself superior to the seasons; and may set at defiance the morning mist and evening damp, the blasts of the east, and the clouds of the south.'

"I make daily excursions on horseback, as well for exercise, as to enjoy the magnificent scenery which surrounds us. Yesterday I looked with rapture upon a fine prospect from La Papa. Far as the eye could reach, extended a gentle, undulating plain, occasionally varied with patches of brush or underwood, and scattered clumps of trees; while in the extreme distance loomed mountains whose indistinct outline mingled with the haze that floated round. Above was a cloudless sky, which is far more pleasant in imagination than in reality, and except in town there was scarcely a human habitation anywhere to be seen. Carthagena is in some sort a city of convents and churches; and these edifices are remarkable for their size and noble style of architecture. Entering next day one of the most noted of them, I found the contents in unison with its external appearance, being enriched and beautified with a vast variety of sacerdotal trinkets, fine tombs and monuments. It is almost impossible to imagine the human intellect sunk so low as to credit the stories of the monks as to the curiosities deposited in the churches, yet the holy fathers have so completely enslaved the minds of the people, that they implicitly believe that they have here a portion of the true cross, some of Christ's garments for which lots were cast, and one of the dice used upon the occasion. O monstrous credulity! wicked imposition! abominable lies!

"Arrived at the quarters of the guide who was to conduct me to my uncle's tomb, I was confronted by a venerable and respectable old man, by whose dignified manner and soldierly bearing I was much impressed. His white beard descended to his waist, and he supported himself upon a staff. Accosting me in English, he stated that he was a native of North Carolina—that his name was Martin, which the inhabitants of Carthagena had converted into Don Martino. When I mentioned the object of my visit, his aged face brightened and his eye sparkled with delight. He said he left North Carolina, October, 1740, with between 200 and 300 American soldiers recruited to take part in the operations against this place. He perfectly recollected my uncle, who had brought his own company eighty-eight strong. The first attack they made on the forts was March 5th, on which day three redoubts were captured, but no further success was obtained and the fleet set sail, the expedition having failed, on the 28th of April.

"The account he gave of my uncle's participation in these operations was this:—On the 5th of April, 1500 men were landed from the fleet, which was commanded by Commodore Dent, and marched around Fort Moncinilla, up a narrow valley, to a house called Grave, to attack La Papa—a half fort—half monastery on the highest hill hereabouts. This force was provided with small arms only. Near La Quinta they came upon a considerable body of the enemy fortified in a defile. These were quickly driven from their works and before our victorious troops, to the monastery of La Papa. Before this fort our men remained all night exposed to the miasma and dews which render the country so fatal to the European constitution. Next morning at four o'clock the entire American force advanced, under my uncle, to attack this strong work, which, had it been properly defended, might have resisted our entire army.

E

Uncle Robert found it abandoned. Mounting the parapet to tear down a Spanish flag, he was mortally wounded by a shot fired by a monk who lingered in a cell. From this wound he died in three hours. Our infuriated soldiers tore the fanatical wretch to pieces, and cast his remains from the ramparts. These are the few simple facts connected with his death, which have been so enlarged and embellished in our domestic traditions.

Martin conducted me to the spot where my uncle lies buried, in the midst of the brave men who perished in this unfortunate expedition. Uncle Robert did not gasp his last breath in a foreign land, " unhousel'd, disappoint'd, unanel'd," as our tradition relates, but was interred with military honours, and his final resting place was marked by a rough stone prepared by the army. This still stands in perfect preservation, guarded by an iron railing—the same placed there by the family. Upon the lower part of the slab I caused these words to be inscribed :—

" *This spot was visited by J. R. P., of Virginia, a nephew of the deceased, July,* 1773. *Light lie the ashes of the dead, and hallowed be the turf that pillows the head of a soldier.*"

"Spanish Town, August, 1773.

"This visit to the last resting place of my lamented uncle cast a gloom over my spirits, from which I did not recover during my stay, and I was glad to leave. The return voyage was soon over and my return known. Among the first who called was Captain Hull, who drove me in his chaise to the course, where I met the world of fashion, including Mrs. and Miss Howe, taking the air. Mrs. Howe informed me that she had issued, some days since, invitations for a soirée, and asked me to excuse a short notice, and give her the pleasure of my company on the next evening. Need I say that I enjoyed the festivities? My favourable impressions of Miss Howe were strengthened. She is a thorough bred, well informed woman, with the instinct, courtesy, and innate grace of a young gentlewoman. Though a little timid and reserved, as what high-bred woman is not at eighteen? she has none of the awkwardness which belongs to the ill-informed, half-bred and vulgar, who in insular communities frequently manage to get into the beau monde. She is quite remarkable in the society here for her ready wit, repartee and wonderful talent for mimicry. She is never, however, betrayed by her wit into sarcasm, nor by her talent for repartee into impertinence. On the contrary, she seems to remember the excellent advice of Lord Lyttleton to the woman he loved and wedded.

> "'Nor make to dangerous wit a vain pretence,
> But simply rest content with common sense;
> For wit, like wine, intoxicates the brain,
> Too strong for feeble woman to sustain.
> Of those who claim it, more than half have none,
> And half of those who have it are undone.'

"Indeed, so far from showing any such propensities, she is, as I am informed by every one, all humility, charity, gentleness, and patient self-control.

"My visit occurs, during what is regarded as the worst season, but I have found the heat mitigated by the breezes that play here, from both land and sea. These blow alternately, the sea breeze during the day, and the land breeze at night. The average of the thermometer is eighty degrees, from July to November. Sometimes it rises in the towns and low lands to ninety degrees, and occasionally in the mountains falls to forty-five degrees. The most pleasant part of the twenty-four hours is at day dawn, before the sun has begun to pour his effulgence over the earth, and before the land breeze has died away. The sea breeze now sets in, coming invariably from the south-east, or from some point ranging from south to east. At first it is very gentle, only slightly rippling the surface of the ocean, and increasing gradually, until it often assumes the strength of a temporary hurricane. The panting and melting inhabitants hail it with a sensation of relief and thankfulness, which can only be known to those whose lot it has been to breathe the oppressive and suffocating atmosphere of southern climes In the afternoon the sea breeze gradually dies away, when both sea and land are locked in the stillness of repose. Were it not for the alternation of trade winds and inland breezes, the West Indies would be wholly unsuited for the European constitution. You are so well informed as to the natural productions that I need only say that every species of fruit and plant flourishes here, as they only do in a tropical climate. The ground is so overloaded that there is scarcely room for the development of the plants. The noble stems of the older trees are almost concealed by the thick drapery of ferns, mosses and orchideous plants, which diffuse through the air the richest odours. The growth of these lovely parasites is encouraged by the moisture of the atmosphere and the shade above, which protects them from the direct rays of the sun. The borders of the numerous streams which descend from the mountains are ornamented with rich verdure and lovely flowers, which blush and bloom under shelter of the wide spreading branches of the mango, mahogany, teak, mimosa, and logwood. The rocks even are covered with creeping plants of every form and colour, yellow, green, and crimson. Indeed the natural endowments of this country are such that it can only be regarded as a terrestrial paradise.

"I must not neglect to add that one of the greatest annoyances is the myriads of ants that everywhere swarm as well within as without doors. The only redeeming feature connected with their presence is the fact that they act as scavengers. Far more disagreeable, however, are the musquitoes, though they are not so large and formidable as those of Carthagena. In that place they are a frightful nuisance, no part of the body indeed is free from their venomous probosces. After a residence of several years in the country they no longer disturb the stranger. As for the blacks they never annoy them here any more than in Virginia; the negro's oily skin seems impervious to their sting. Some of the lizards I have seen frisking across the country roads are two feet long, and resemble young alligators. They are not venomous, and the negroes consider their flesh a delicacy; it is white and resembles that of the chicken. There are many other insects, reptiles, birds and animals; but this is no place, were it possible to me, even to give a list of them. I shall content myself with what I have said of the country, its productions, &c., from which you will observe that I have consulted my senses and not my imagination, and sought to describe things as I have seen them. I have met with no 'basilisks that destroy with their eyes, nor crocodiles who shed tears while devouring their prey,' and my cataracts fall from rocks without deafening the neighbouring inhabitants. In what I have said I have endeavoured indeed to follow the course of the Portuguese traveller, who says in the Preface to his travels.*

" 'The reader will here find no regions cursed with irremediable barrenness, or blest with spontaneous fecundity; no perpetual gloom, or unceasing sunshine; nor are the nations here described either devoid of all sense of humanity, or consummate in all private or social virtues. Here are no Hottentots without religious policy or articulate language; no Chinese perfectly polite, and completely skilled in all sciences; he will discover, what will always be discovered by a diligent and impartial inquirer, that wherever human nature is to be found, there is a mixture of vice and virtue, a contest of passion and reason; and that the Creator doth not appear partial in his distribution, but has balanced in most countries, their particular inconveniences by particular favours.' "

Annie Howe, to whom he refers so enthusiastically in this epistle, was then eighteen and among all the beautiful women of Spanish Town, the palm of beauty was readily

* This preface was written by Dr. Johnson.

yielded to her. Her features were faultlessly regular, and the sparkle of diamond brightness in her eyes, sufficed to illumine "a boundless contiguity of shade." Her studies had been directed with such care that they imparted to her mind a masculine strength, which elevated her above all the common dangers of that period, when a woman enters society. She was noble in her sentiments, frank and unaffected in her manners.

In a subsequent page the reader will hear more of this interesting young lady and her family, which was, indeed, one of the most respectable and influential in the colony.

CHAPTER VII.

HE SAILS FOR NEW ORLEANS.—THE MISSISSIPPI RIVER.—NEW ORLEANS.—THE INHABITANTS.—HISTORICAL COUP D'ŒIL.—GENERAL D'ULOA.—COUNT O'REILLY.—JUDICIAL MURDERS AND CONFISCATIONS.—THE GOVERNOR AND HIS ENTERTAINMENT.

It will be quite obvious to the reader, from the contents as well as the date of the following letter to his father, that several are missing between it and that contained in the last preceding chapter. The missing letters refer, however, exclusively to commercial matters, and their loss can, therefore, be better borne, unpleasant as it is nevertheless. The letter incorporated herein, is dated at Tichfield, Jamaica, August 20th, 1773, but was concluded in New Orleans, on the 25th of the following month. It contains an interesting account of his voyage from Jamaica; and of the capital of Lower Louisiana; and is followed by a hiatus of nine months in the correspondence. During which stirring period, the most exciting events in this history occur, as will appear from the sequel.

" I secured passage for New Orleans for myself and manservant, Charles Lucas, whom I have thought it prudent to engage, as in case of illness, or other misadventure, his services may be of great value. He is what is called a

Mestizoes, or the son of an Englishman, by a native Maroon, or Indian, and possesses, in a modified form, the physical peculiarities of the North American savage. Having the copper skin, small, fierce black, penetrating eyes, barely separated by the nose, round forehead, high cheek bones, prominent sharp hooked nose, elongated skull, small mouth, and thin compressed lips of the Virginia Catawbas. His countenance bespeaks shrewdness, ingenuity and resolution. Though, by no means, a physical beauty, he possesses many fine points—is tall, muscular and bony, has a good figure indicative of great hardihood, strength and activity. His shoulders are expanded to an enormous breadth, he is entirely unencumbered with flesh, and the texture of his limbs is Herculean. He has, however, many other good qualities of far greater value than good looks, among them honesty and fidelity, and comes to me with the highest recommendations from two Tichfield gentlemen as a man on whose fidelity the utmost reliance can be placed. With a Jamaica gentleman he visited England, in his capacity of valet, five years since. He seemed exceedingly anxious too, to visit Virginia, where some of his friends, relations indeed, reside in the Chotank settlement. When he reaches the Colony, I think it most probable he will remain, for reasons, I will hereafter explain. If he turns out as well as I hope and as I am induced to believe he will, he may become a valuable acquisition to you, and be made very useful at Stoney Hill, as a kind of sub-overseer, to look after the affairs of the plantation. It was with some reference to this ulterior object, that I engaged him, or I should rather say his anxiety to go, and my impression that he might be made of service to you after his brief engagement with myself, induced me to discard any objections which occurred to me against taking him, and to engage his services. Among his other accomplishments, he has an accurate knowledge of the Spanish language, which will be of much assistance to me while in Louisiana and Florida. I have indulged in a more lengthy description of my valet than probably, the inferior merit of the matter deserves, especially as I am in the midst of objects of greater interest. But I have always thought, however personal appearance may be in the eye of moral philosophy a very inferior consideration, and mind the proper study of man; yet in describing a person or people, I cannot think it altogether unnecessary to include his, or their personal appearance, as I think there exists a stronger analogy between the person and the mind of man, than is generally perceived.

"But we are about to be off, to turn our backs upon this lovely isle, where I have received so much kindness, and passed so many happy hours. I shall probably never see it again. Sad thought! One of my greatest pleasures through life will be that I have visited it, one of my profoundest sorrows, that I shall never see it again. I shall never forget its beautiful plantations of cane, its orange groves, its native vineyards, its green vallies, and lofty mountains, the hospitable men and lovely women of this *vrai* land of love and romance!"

"On board the 'Ocean Wave,' off the mouth of the Mississippi,
September 1st, 1773.

"This letter was commenced a few hours previous to sailing, with a view to continuing it on ship board and posting from New Orleans. Our voyage thus far has been without incident We came in sight of land this forenoon, the day fine, with a clear, serene sky. The shore lies flat and presents no interesting features. As we approach, the land seems to rise higher on the surface of the water. Much sand and mud is deposited near the mouth of the river, occasionally obstructing the passage, not, however, for any length of time, as the rapid current of this mighty river soon forces a new channel to the sea. Our progress however, is delayed, as we are forced to take frequent soundings. As there are no light-houses on the coast, we necessarily proceed with the utmost caution."

"New Orleans, September 25th, 1773.

"We arrived off the mouth of the Mississippi the night of the 21st, and passing Mud Cape, proceeded up the river with a favourable wind, reaching New Orleans the same day. To my surprise, I found almost all the inhabitants French—few of them even speaking Spanish, and all entertaining a prejudice against the Castilian race. I was equally surprised to find that though French, all their feelings were kind towards the English. No better evidence can be given of this than the fact that there is a penalty of 500 dollars for admitting a British subject into their houses, unless the government is immediately advised of the fact. Notwithstanding this heavy penalty, the people receive the English colonists warmly to their habitations, extending to them every hospitality. New Orleans contains 12,000 inhabitants and is the seat of government of Lower Louisiana, and garrisoned by Spanish troops. From the period when France ceded the territory to Spain, no friendship has existed between the French and Spanish inhabitants, and at one time it was manifested in open rebellion. When the Spanish, about the year 1765, shortly after the cession of the territory from France, sought to introduce their commercial regulations, the French inhabitants rose in mass, seized Monsieur Aubry, who was then commandant under the French Government, but had accepted office with the Spaniards, and threw him into prison. On the 30th of October, 1768, they expelled the Governor, Don Antonio d'Uloa, and all the Spanish officers. These set sail, and shortly after arrived at the Havannah. Only one Spanish vessel now remained in the port of New Orleans and this was unfit for sea. Heavily armed, she continued at her moorings, prepared to resist any attack from the shore. She was unmolested by the insurgents, who met in public meeting, and after taking counsel as to their present condition and future prospects, decided to despatch four agents to Paris, to ask the protection and intercession of the French government, for a redress of their grievances. Before tidings were received of the reception of these diplomatic agents, a Spanish expedition, which was fitted out at the Havannah, consisting of four men of war and several transports, with 3,000 troops under command of General Count O'Reilly arrived in the Mississippi and took up its position opposite the city. The " City fathers," to prevent unnecessary effusion of blood, immediately and unconditionally surrendered the place. O'Reilly took possession and promised to administer summary punishment upon the most guilty. Thirty of the leading citizens were seized, tried by court martial and shot the same day. The estates of these and 200 others were confiscated. Such was the terror inspired by these acts, that the inhabitants gave in their unconditional submission. Their outward acquiescence to Spanish authority was thus secured, but hatred of their conquerors rankled in their bosoms and continues to the present time. The French detest nothing so much as their Spanish rulers, and daily become more bold in expressing their desire of re-union with France. If this is impossible, they would prefer British authority to Spanish tyranny. So deep and general is this feeling, that I am satisfied, a single company of English troops, aided by the French population, could throw off the Spanish yoke. Much the larger portion of the inhabitants of Lower Louisiana are French. The only Spaniards are proud, lazy officials and miserable troops, who constitute the garrison. These indolent officials and drunken troops affect the greatest airs of superiority, and look down with contempt upon the French inhabitants.

" The streets of the city are laid out at right angles, and the houses are generally one storey high, yet many of them are handsome and substantial, and surrounded by pleasant flower gardens. The banks of the river are steep, almost perpendicular, and the river so deep that the largest vessels lie broadside to the shore, where they are secured by cables fastened to the trees. Opposite the city the river is about 1,000 yards wide. There is but one current, that downward, to the sea. The ocean tide does not reach the city. Indeed the force of the current of this mighty river is so extraordinary, that there is scarcely any tide at its mouth, and its turbid waters may be detected for many leagues in the gulf. One striking peculiarity of the river is that its depth increases as you ascend; another, that when its waters overflow their banks below the river Ibberville, they never return again within them. These peculiarities distinguish it from every other known river in the world.

"The land on the river banks is of extraordinary fertility, so much so, that reeds grow upon the high lands. This, I think, is unexampled; at least, I have nowhere seen reeds growing, save on the Mississippi, unless in low, marshy ground. The annual overflow leaves upon the shores a slime, similar to the deposits of the Nile, which insures the fertility of Egypt. The principal crop is indigo, which is the staple production of the territory; and I am told that it is produced in larger quantities from the same extent of land than anywhere else in the world. Its good qualities are also increased by the amazing fertility of the soil. The 'richer' the land, the better the indigo,' is a Louisiana proverb. The climate and soil are equally well adapted to the growth of the sugar cane. The manufacture of sugar, however, requiring many labourers and much expensive machinery, has not been largely engaged in. The sugar they have already manufactured in small quantities is excellent, indeed is unsurpassed, as I have had, since my arrival, every opportunity of knowing, having used none other. Indian corn, wheat, tobacco, and, in fact, all the ordinary products of Virginia flourish on the Lower Mississippi. I am satisfied if this territory belonged to His Majesty's dominions, there would be a large emigration to it from the northern colonies. Holding the upper waters or tributaries of the river, and having no other outlet to the sea, it is of the first importance that we should acquire Louisiana. It is the key to the northwestern part of the continent—the only channel by which that extensive region communicates with the sea. I am so impressed with the value and importance—indeed, the necessity— of this acquisition, that I think England's motto in reference to it should be 'Peaceably, if I can—forcibly, if I must.' I apprehend there is some danger, from my warmth on this subject, of your voting me a land pirate, *per se*, a wilful violator of the seventh commandment. Perhaps I may be but I view it in the light of a necessity, as something not only essential to the prosperity of His Majesty's colonies, but as absolutely necessary to our defence. An enemy entering the Mississippi and ascending the Ohio, would cut our country in twain—separate the east and west, and take us front and rear. Can we ever allow this? My instincts and reason respond never. I am satisfied, at some future time, Louisiana must belong to those who own the country bathed by the Upper Mississippi, and enriched by the numberless streams it receives; Providence seems, by the system of rivers, lakes, mountains, &c., to have designed the vast region lying between the Canadian lakes and the Mexican Gulf for one country. If I be not mistaken in this view, sooner or later, it will come under one authority, either that of His Majesty and his successors, or as constituting one grand Anglo-American empire.

"Shortly after my arrival, I delivered a letter I bore to Messrs. Willing and Morris, the most important merchants of the city, and through whom it is supplied with flour, principally imported from Philadelphia. They enjoy a monopoly of this trade, or the exclusive privilege of importing flour from the King of Spain. Every hospitality and attention has been shown me by these excellent and enterprising gentlemen. They informed me that it was the etiquette of the place to call upon the Governor, and one of them, when I signified my purpose to go through this form, proposed accompanying me. We accordingly called the following day upon His Excellency, who kept us some time 'dancing attendance in his anteroom.' I felt indignant at his conduct, but Mr. Morris took it very coolly. He told me it resulted first from the inflated pride of the Spaniards, and, secondly, from their jealousy of strangers, whom they had always sought in the most narrow-minded, illiberal, and jealous spirit to exclude from and keep in ignorance of their American settlements. It was this spirit which induced them to place many vexatious restrictions upon trade and commerce, by which the price of European goods was so much enhanced that none but the wealthy could use them—unless, as was some time the case, they were obtained through French and Dutch smugglers, who drove a prosperous, though illicit trade. The Governor is not, like Cæsar's wife, above suspicion, and he is thought to gain 30,000 dollars a-year by conniving at various abuses—these are here called his perquisites of office. While Mr. Morris was proceeding with his narrative, a servant appeared and conducted us to the Governor's presence. He received us quite differently from what I had anticipated. I expected hauteur and formality, but received only civility and kindness. If he entertained any distrust of me as a British subject, he disguised it effectually, seeming to grow more friendly as our interview continued. He inquired for my lodgings, where he called the next day, and left an invitation to dinner. Mr. Morris having also been invited, we subsequently attended, and though it was somewhat stiff and formal, it was not His Excellency's fault. He has given me so many proofs of kindness by his generous attentions, that I think him one of the most amiable and excellent of men—the best of Spaniards."

CHAPTER VIII.

HE SAILS FOR FLORIDA BUT IS CAPTURED BY THE SPANIARDS AND CAR-
RIED TO NEW MEXICO.—MARCHES EIGHTY-NINE DAYS UP THE RIO DEL
NORTE TO SANTA FE, WHERE HE IS IMPRISONED AND TREATED WITH
INHUMAN BARBARITY.

I SHALL not anticipate my grandfather by making any lengthy reference to a series of remarkable adventures, which finally terminated by his arrival in St. Louis, but allow him to relate his own story, which he does in the three next letters, dated at that place on the 10th, 12th, and 13th of May, 1774. St. Louis was at that period in the occupancy of the French, and was a simple military station and outpost of the fur-traders, whose operations extended almost to the eastern base of the Rocky Mountains. The head-quarters of these adventurous and enterprising men was at Detroit, the present capital of the State of Michigan. A chain of stockade forts[*] con-

[*] These stockade forts were thus constructed: The plan having been marked out, a trench three feet in depth was dug, within which the trunks of trees, or palisades, each generally about a foot in diameter and eighteen feet high, were firmly planted, a platform of boards about six feet high being built all round the interior for the men to stand on when firing through loop holes cut in the palisades. Cannon if used were mounted on the angles. These little forts—generally square and the sides rarely more than two hundred feet long—not only furnished their garrisons with sufficient protection against the savages who possessed no artillery, but when strengthened by earthen embankments

nected the French settlements in Canada with Louisiana, by way of Detroit and St. Louis.

"I hasten, upon my arrival here, *en route* for Virginia, from a long captivity among the Spaniards in New Mexico, and an extraordinary journey through the wilderness to this place, to inform you of my safety. I would content myself with this simple announcement, if I could thereby place this letter the sooner in your hands. As this is impossible, I shall employ my leisure while recruiting my health and strength, by writing you an accurate and faithful narrative of the leading incidents and extraordinary vicissitudes of fortune which have chequered the whole series of adventures which have befallen me since my letters of August, 1773. Under the pressure of accumulated afflictions, my mind has been ceaselessly goaded by the thought of the gloomy depression, the harrowing grief my absence and supposed death must have inflicted upon my dear mother and yourself. My

and surrounded by a *fosse*, as was usually the case, were proof against the small and inferior guns used at that time in the interior, by the English. The North American Indians are not only very ingenious in their plans for surprising an enemy, but are equally so in the art of concealing their own presence from their foes. One of their contrivances is worth describing. During the winter, when artificial warmth is necessary to them, yet when a fire upon the surface of the ground would by its light discover their position at a distance, they dig holes in the ground, from four to six feet in diameter and somewhat deeper. In the bottom of these they make a fire of charcoal cut from the burnt logs lying in the forest—of which there is always a supply as the Indians annually burn the woods to frighten the game from their recesses, and to promote the growth of grass—and this charcoal, while it warms, does not discover them by its smoke, light, flame, or sparks. At night they sleep round these fire-pits, lying upon their backs with their legs hanging down in the holes, as it is an essential point with the savages to keep their feet warm, and their heads cool. They thus secure strength of body for the combat, and clear wits for the council; in fact, without being acquainted with the works of the celebrated physician Arbuthnot, these untutored Indians have, by a process of their own, arrived at what the Scottish Æsculapius deemed the sum and substance of all medical knowledge, and condensed in his own pithy apothegm "keep the head cool, the feet warm, and the bowels open."

very heart has been wrung by this sorrow. All is well, however, that ends well, and now that I have emerged from the 'sea of trouble' which threatened to overwhelm me and am approaching home, my spirits are elastic and my mind and body re-invigorated. Insensibly I am recovering from, if not forgetting the barbarities and cruelties I have suffered.

"Immediately upon my arrival at this place I was met by a Mr. Malet, an English gentleman residing here, who had heard of my coming from an Osage warrior, who preceded our canoe down the river. In the most kind and hospitable manner, he insisted upon my living at his house, instead of the inn, where I was proceeding to take up my quarters. His manner of asking was so engaging, interesting, and impressive, that I found it impossible to refuse him. Under his hospitable roof I shall remain while here, and from its shelter I write you this letter. It is a plain house, erected of timber, but the most unaffected hospitality and generous benevolence invites and spreads the board, and politeness and affability preside over all. Never shall I forget it—never shall I think of it without gratitude and esteem.

"The day after last writing from New Orleans we set sail from that place, bound for St. Augustine in East Florida. Our vessel was the 'Swan,' Captain Jones. No adventure overtook us worth mentioning till five days thereafter, when in the Gulf of Mexico. Here, the winds becoming adverse, we were driven from our course. These gales soon increased to the fury of a hurricane, during which our sails were split in shreds, and our mainmast went overboard. Had we been left to ourselves, we must have perished. When, however, our destruction seemed impending we were descried by a Spanish vessel which hove in sight, bound from Havannah to the Rio Grande or Rio del Norte, in the province of New Mexico. We hailed this vessel as a deliverance, a special mark of the favour of Providence to rescue us from a watery grave, and made every signal of distress to attract her attention. The Spaniard bore down upon us, and, sending hands on board, succeeded in saving crew and vessel. We soon learned that we had been snatched from the jaws of death only for a probably more terrible fate. The Spaniards, to cover their piratical designs, now charged that we were French enemies, and, without more ado, the vessel and everything in it was declared confiscated to the use of the King of Spain. With the rest, I was robbed of every valuable. Putting a few hands upon the 'Swan,' they soon repaired the damage she sustained from the tempest. This was easily done now, as the storm had partially subsided, and, when completed, the two ships proceeded together towards the Rio del Norte. The captain of the Spanish ship, pretending he was short of provisions, scarcely supplied us with sufficient food to sustain life. To every protestation which was made as to our true character as British subjects, they turned a deaf ear, and that they might not be annoyed by importunities, they placed us below in irons. To every complaint we made for food, they replied that the stock on the 'Swan' was damaged and had been thrown overboard. Several days after this event we arrived at the mouth of the Rio del Norte, and were landed. Three of the crew of the 'Swan' were so reduced by disease and starvation, that they died within five hours of our arrival. We were here placed in the hands of the Spanish authorities, who imprisoned us in forts made of bricks dried in the sun, while the vessels proceeded up the river. The food here doled out to us in insufficient quantities, consisted only of a small measure of parched corn and a little fruit. The officials had the grace to intimate, as they were scarce of meat, if we chose to butcher, we might eat a lame mule, which broke down on a journey from the interior, and was left there to die by its owner, a fur-trader. In our emaciated and starving condition we felt there was no alternative and accepted their bounty. The mule was soon slaughtered and some of its tough flesh dressed. In my then famished condition, however, I thought I had never eaten anything so savoury and delicious. Strange as it may seem, the flesh of this animal, though only seasoned with coarse salt, agreed with us and appeared to infuse into our frames new strength and vigour.* We were confined at this point a fortnight, our party of nine living the while upon the flesh of the animal. The preparations of our captors to conduct us to the interior were then completed. For the first time we were informed that we must proceed on foot a journey of eighty-nine days to Santa Fé, the capital of the province of New Mexico. The longer I knew and the more familiarized I became to my Indian servant, the more satisfied was I of my good fortune in having engaged his services. His character disclosed much better traits than his first appearance bespoke, and I began to have perfect confidence in him.

"Up to this period my travels had laid through countries under the authority of Europeans, their laws and customs; and consequently little presented itself respecting human nature of such novelty as to excite admiration, or awaken curiosity. In Jamaica, at Carthagena, in Louisiana, in fact, in all the various places through which I had passed, a certain parity of sentiment, arising from the one great substratum, Christianity, gave the same general colouring to all the scenes, however they might differ from each other in their various shadings. I was now, however, about to enter an almost unexplored region, and to contemplate man under a variety of forms and complications entirely different from those to which habit had familiarized my mind. I therefore contemplated with pleasant

---

* The exertions of the Society in Paris for encouraging *hippophagy*, or the use of horse flesh, have proved that it is highly nutritious; and in the hands of a French cook, has a delicate and delicious *gout* or flavour. There are now (1867) in Paris eighteen establishments for the sale of horse flesh, the two largest being in the Rue de Navarin, and the Rue du Commerce. Sausages and horse-steaks *aux pommes de terre* are greatly patronized by the poor.

excitement, the prospect of travelling, notwithstanding the terrible circumstances under which I should accomplish it, as a prisoner in chains, hundreds of miles through the immense and almost trackless wilds of a country inhabited by savage tribes, and semi-civilized Spanish half-breeds, without the consolation of any other companions in my journey, than a few miserable partners of my imprisonment, fatigues, and perils.

"The following morning we set forth upon this long journey, under an escort of twenty wild bandit-looking Mexican horsemen. Manacled and ironed together, two and two, we made the first day in the scorching sun twenty-six miles through a sandy desert, covered with cactus, endemis, yuccas, helianthoides and wormwood. My feelings, which were altogether of the most unpleasant kind, served as a stimulus to my mind, and increased my anxiety to get forward. I therefore pushed on as rapidly as if I anticipated life and liberty, instead of assassination at the end of my journey. To my no small satisfaction I was bound to my servant Charles. I preferred the society of this faithful half-breed, to the coarse companionship of a filthy French sailor. My mind was under the dominion of a gloomy presentiment, was, as Shakspeare emphatically says, "A phantasm, or a hideous dream—and my little state of man suffered, as it were, the nature of an insurrection." Such was the chaos within me, that I seemed beyond the power of discriminate reflection. I found in my case, as I believe it is universal, that human sufferings, like all other things, find their vital principal exhausted, and their extinction accelerated by overgrowth; and that, at the moment when man thinks himself most miserable, a benignant Providence is preparing relief in some form or other for him. So it was with me, and I found the labour and fatigue of the journey something which beguiled me insensibly of the gloomy contemplations in which I was previously absorbed, and afforded my tortured mind a temporary suspension of pain.

"At night, we were confined in the stable of a small farmer, and guarded by sentinels. The Mexicans knowing we could not continue our journey without proper food, supplied us freely with Indian corn meal, from which we baked bread in the hot ashes, and jerked beef. Travelling in this way, we proceeded up the river for three weeks. About this time, two of our party, overcome by fatigue and sickness, (for they had been suffering with fever and dysentery,) fell insensible on the ground from sun stroke. Here they were left to expire in the broiling sun. Fearing, no doubt, that all of us would die in this way, and that they would thus lose the reward promised for safely conducting us to the capital, they hired, this day, seven pack-horses for our use. We were each set upon a horse, on a wooden pack-saddle, and our arms tied behind us, and our legs under the horses' belly. Then placing a bell around the horses' neck, and taking the bridle, they drove us before them for ten days. We were thus preserved from slow death, as we were from immediate slaughter at the hands of these bandits, by the hope of reward for our safe delivery in Santa Fé. During this time they did not fail to insult us in the most wanton manner, and visit upon us the greatest ignominies and most unaccountable cruelties. There was no restriction to deter them from indulging their bad passions in this manner. As they had only engaged our horses for ten days, they determined to make the most of them, and we only halted for their necessary refreshment—I mean the refreshment of the bandits and horses—for they gave us nothing beyond our allowance of bread and dried beef. Every night we were compelled to lie upon the bare ground, but fortuuately the wet season had not set in, and we only suffered from the heavy dews. In this inhuman, barbarous manner, we travelled 350 miles, passing many places, where, with the utmost difficulty, our guard prevented the savage inhabitants from murdering us in cold blood. Though they preserved our lives for the sake of the reward, they made no effort to protect us from the most cruel and mortifying insults and maltreatment at every inhabited place where we halted. Several times we were actually exhibited to the people, men, women, and children, as a public show, and as if belonging to a different species of animal from the *genus homo.* The most inveterate hatred of and prejudice existed against the French, who were supposed to cherish designs of conquest, and a disposition to exterminate the Spanish race. Besides hearing that some of our party were Protestants, their religious hatred was aroused against these, and everywhere we were called 'hogs;' they sneered at and abused us *ad libitum* and *ad nauseum.* They hissed at us ' *Crees in Dios !*' ' *Crees en este !*' ' *Crees en este !*' ' *No ! no !*' ' *Ah Judio !*' ' *Barbaro, Bruto !*' ' *Protestante !*' ' *Puerco !*' ' *Voia al los infernos !*' which is in English : 'Do you believe in God?' 'Do you believe in this?' 'Do you believe in this!' 'No! no!' 'Ah Jew!' 'Barbarian Protestant !' 'Hog !' 'Go to hell !' Often they approached near, seeking an opportunity to stab us with their daggers *por amor de Dios.* Our mercenary guides alone preserved us from the stilettos of the mob, but I already entertained apprehensions that the pious fathers of the church would, when a favourable occasion presented, conscientiously consign us to the inquisition, and then to the flames. How different was the end ! Those we expected to ruin became our deliverers.

Giving up the pack horses at the end of ten days, we continued our journey on foot, for sixteen more, until the 29th of November, 1774, when we arrived at a kind of fort or settlement on the river, six days' march from Santa Fé. Our shoes, with the exception of a single pair, were gone several days previous to this—one pair after another disappearing, until no one possessed any but my servant Charles, who continued to bear up, in the midst of our sufferings, with the indomitable pluck and spirit of the American Indian. He often insisted on my using his shoes, going the length of taking them off and walking in his naked feet, saying he would not use them while I had none. I refused persistently to appropriate them, being unwilling in our then miserable condition, to accept such a favour from a human being, in no better condition than myself. When we marched in the Spanish fort bare footed and ragged, Charles still carried his shoes, to the no small surprise of the Spaniards, who were ignorant of the noble motive which caused this singular conduct. This simple act of a poor, uninformed, half-breed, had more of the true and essential spirit of Christianity in it, than half the ostentatious charity of the world. It was based upon kindness, disinterestedness and delicacy, and struck me more forcibly than all the acts of benificence that I ever met with.

"For some reason, which I never understood, we delayed at this place seven days. We were all confined in one room, under a strong guard, suffering daily every species of insult, and in danger and dread of being murdered every night. Crowds of half-savage Spaniards assembled daily about our prison to denounce vengeance against us, and to launch at us every bitter reproach, every filthy epithet and every horrible imprecation in their vocabulary. They boasted too of their patience and forbearance, which fortunately enabled them to refrain from annihilating us at once. After this delay, we resumed our journey, and though I was suffering from dysentery and consequent weakness, and my whole body was lacerated with pain, and my mind distracted with doubts and difficulties, arrived with the residue of our dispirited party in Santa Fé. The last 300 miles of our journey was through a beautiful and fertile country, to the charms of which, however, the agony of my feelings rendered me almost insensible. In Santa Fé we were delivered to the authorities, who subjected us to a rigid and barbarous imprisonment. My feet were swollen, blistered, and bleeding, and gave me such intolerable pain, that for nights together I could not sleep.

My prostration was such that I could not have gone another day's journey, though life and liberty had been my reward. My dysentery continued, and I found myself seized with a violent bilious fever, here called a seasoning or acclimatizing fever, which brought me to the verge of death. I had no nurse but my faithful Charles, no food fit for a sick person. Nature and a good constitution were my only physicians and medicines, save a few simple drugs, which were clandestinely conveyed to me with directions for their use by Father Lopez, a Catholic priest, whom Charles (who, by-the-bye, is a Roman Catholic in faith,) had managed, during the priest's visit to the prison, to interest in my fate. My illness made me quite delirious and helpless for ten days, and it was five weeks before I was out of danger. For some time after this I was so weak and low, that I had scarcely strength to walk across the room. The jailor's daughter, Annetta, who was now much interested in our behalf, by the intercession of the priest, privately furnished me with suitable food for a convalescent—such as broths, fruit and the like, and I regained my strength with rapidity. You can scarcely believe this possible, when I tell you that the iron and wooden doors of our cell were constantly locked and chained, no one even in the prison being allowed to speak to Charles or myself—(we were alone in the ward,)—nor to answer any question if we called to them; that I was on my recovery, restricted from the use of pen, ink, and paper, and allowed not the smallest communication with any human being but my poor servant; that I had no chair, table, bed, blanket or straw, and was obliged to lie upon the bare floor with a billet of wood under my head. Sometimes we were left by the jailor two or three days together without food or drink. But for the good priest and his young female confederate, who came to our cell in the midst of night, carrying her jar of water and her basket of supplies, we must have perished. For eight weeks I remained extremely lame and ill, without having changed my linen or clothes, save on one occasion, when I was supplied by Father Lopez. Indeed, it is strange how human nature could support all I endured. The climate, however, aided greatly in my recovery—the air of Santa Fé being dry, pure, and bracing. The heat in summer is not so intense as on the gulf, or in the same latitude on the Atlantic, and is generally not greater than in the upper districts of Virginia, nor is the cold so great in winter, as in Virginia. The mornings and evenings, even in the hottest weather, are always cool and pleasant. During the winter, snow lies upon the high peaks of the Rocky mountains, but seldom remains longer than a few hours in the valleys and lower districts. No diseases have appeared since the settlement of the province by Spaniards, which can be said to be peculiar to the climate and country. The seasoning or bilious fever is only known in the country south of the 30th degree of latitude. My recovery from it is doubtless, in great measure, due to the rapidity with which we travelled north from the unhealthy districts on the Lower Rio del Norte. I feel, from my experience at Santa Fé, that the chances of life are considerably more in our favour there than in the most healthy parts of the continent east of the Rocky mountains. Colds, which are sometimes taken during the winter, never prove fatal without the greatest neglect. The seasons are mild and agreeable, the atmosphere constantly pure and elastic; and the sky clear, unclouded and brilliant.

"But I must proceed with my narrative. Every night of my confinement in that dreary mansion of wretchedness and misery at Santa Fé, my sleep was disturbed with the most dreadful sounds and horrible noises. These proceeded from the clanking of chains, the rattling of massy keys, the creaking of iron doors upon their rusty hinges, the resounding of bolts and bars, and above all the shocking screams and howlings of the unhappy wretches confined in this frightful den. If the racking pain and parching thirst of my fever had allowed me any sleep, I could not have enjoyed it for the frightful noises, which constantly broke upon the stillness of the night. I was much agitated too at this moment by learning that Captain Jones, who was confined in an adjoining ward, had committed suicide. I attributed this horrible act to his protracted sufferings of mind and body, but could find no excuse, but insanity, for such a deed. If ever despair approached me, it was during my prostration in this cruel situation. I felt my life departing from me inch by inch, and even if spared by disease, could we hope to escape assassination. I thoroughly comprehended the blood-thirsty dispositions, the vindictive barbarity of our captors. The reward once paid for our safe delivery in Santa Fé, I knew our lives depended entirely upon their whims and caprices. Nevertheless my resolution did not abandon me. I summoned to my aid religion and philosophy, and while I could not understand why I was so much afflicted, firmly believed that all my calamities were brought upon me by an allwise and merciful providence as a beneficial trial, as it were as an exercise of my virtue. Composing myself as far as was possible, I determined to await the result with patient fortitude. My efforts to bear myself with a steady and perpetual serenity, exercised the most beneficial influence upon my faithful servant, Charles, who was so far overcome, that he occasionally gave way to something like despair. The vague hints of our escape or receiving succour, which I occasionally let fall, merely for the purpose of reviving his strength and hopes, broke like flashes of lightning through the gloomy clouds which enveloped his soul, and kept up a kind of daylight in his mind. Still further to benefit him, I spoke of Captain Jones' suicide as the act of a coward, with no dependence upon himself and no faith in God. I sought to elevate Charles' sentiments, to so regulate his mind that trust and hopefulness might become permanent parts of his disposition. I asked him to remember what obligations we were under to Providence for the incalculable blessings we enjoyed, and not to forget that the visitations, which sometimes overtook and almost crushed us to the earth, are often dispensations of mercy, sent to try and purify us. I said we should meet them with composure, and thus co-operate with providence in its designs, and not provoke further displeasure by querulous discontent and presumptuous doubts. In other words, dear father, I sought to impress in my poor way upon my excellent Charles some of the moral lessons you have so often inculcated by your teachings and example, and which my experience has taught me to be founded in wisdom—that wisdom whose "ways are ways of pleasantness, and all whose paths are peace."

"After several weeks' illness, I felt my fever abate and the worst symptoms of the disorder disappear. As I slowly regained my bodily strength, I recovered the full tone and vigour of my mind; I felt my spirits increase, my resolution become more firm, my hopes more sanguine, and while scarcely able to make on foot the tour of my chamber, commenced revolving plans for extricating myself from prison. There is a spring, an elasticity in every man's mind, of which the owner is rarely, very rarely conscious, because fortunately the occasions seldom occur in which it can be brought to the proof. My deplorable condition even now, and the earnest intercession in my behalf of Father Lopez and the jailor's daughter, moved the iron heart of that terrible man to pity; and Ximines said if I would make application to the Governor for the privilege of walking during certain hours in the grounds, he would see that His Excellency received the petition. He observed that though ordered not to allow me pen, ink, or paper, he would send me a pencil and card. Accordingly I made my application to the Governor for this privilege for myself and my fellow prisoners, in Spanish, dictated by my servant and inscribed upon the back of the ace of diamonds. Much to my surprise the Governor ordered me to be brought before him, and to my greater surprise behaved towards me very politely. He made me many apologies, through his inter-

preter, for the past, and promised me better treatment for
the future. He requested me to give a full account of
myself and my connection with the 'Swan.' This I did,
claiming that I was unjustly imprisoned, whatever might
have been the character of the vessel on which I was taken.
I declared, however, my perfect conviction—in fact my
positive knowledge—that the vessel was the *bond fide* property of British subjects trading to and from New Orleans,
and was not the property of French enemies of the King of
Spain. In consideration of which facts I asked that the
whole of us should be liberated, and as we were in a distant
and almost uninhabited country, without money, friends,
or resources, that we should be supplied with the means of
reaching our homes. I further added that if so disposed
of by His Excellency, we would abandon any claim we had
against the King of Spain for damages resulting from illegal
seizure and false imprisonment, for robbery and ill-treat-
ment. I made bold to add further that our fate could not
be always concealed, and that when known would lead to
the summary punishment of all those by whom we had
suffered. That dead or alive we would be avenged by our
government, and I suggested that all who had injured us
ought to prepare for the wrath against the day of wrath.
When I had proceeded thus far, His Excellency seemed
fatigued and terminated the interview. I was reconducted
to prison, and notwithstanding all the fair promises of the
Governor, left in the same situation as formerly. The
gaoler in fact told me, some days later, through Charles,
that my speech to His Excellency had greatly offended
that august dignitary. Annetta, the daughter, however,
continued her hospitalities to us, and I now learned from
Charles that though only fifteen years of age, she cherished
a secret passion for him, which he returned: that during
my absence at the Governor's they had a conversation and
had sworn eternal fidelity to each other, and that Annetta
had promised if we could effect our escape from prison to
fly with us to 'other lands.'

"Three days after my interview with the Governor, the gaoler produced a paper, which he said was sent to me to sign, after which I would be permitted to go at large in the grounds, attended by my servant. He further said His Excellency had held a conversation with Father Lopez, who actively interested himself in my behalf, and that His Excellency was anxious to atone for the former severity of my imprisonment, by granting me any ameliorations not inconsistent with his duty to government. Upon having the paper translated to me by Charles, I ascertained that it contained an acknowledgment that the 'Swan' was a French vessel, engaged in illegal traffic, and that I was upon her in defiance of the laws of His Catholic Majesty the King of Spain, as also that we were properly or legally imprisoned, and had been treated with tenderness and humanity during our captivity. Made acquainted with the contents of the paper, I refused to sign it upon any terms. For three days it was presented to me for signature, and several threats used to induce me to subscribe my name. I persisted in my refusal, whereupon they recommenced their barbarities. Wooden doors were put up against our windows to exclude the light and so as not to admit fresh air, we were not allowed the use of pen, ink and paper, which was furnished me during the time they were endeavouring to get me to sign the paper; no one whatever was permitted to see or speak to us, and for a week we were as effectually excluded from the whole world as if we had been in our graves. At this very time, however, a kind Providence was preparing relief for us, thus verifying the old adage 'When distress is greatest, God is nearest.' At the end of the seventh day Annetta managed to fetch us at midnight a jug of water and some coarse provisions, but for which we must have perished. Next day the good priest visited us, and seeing the wretched condition to which we were reduced, and despairing of our lives if we continued longer in this confinement, he induced Charles, who was a jesuit, to sign the paper. Charles also, without my knowledge, appended my name.

Our windows were now opened, and we were allowed the free use of the grounds for two hours during the day; these were hot, nasty and suffocating, and under the constant inspection of two sentinels. The indulgence, however, was so grateful to me, after my prison life, that I rapidly improved in strength. About this time the gaoler brought in an enormous bill against me for diet, candles, attendance, &c. I refused to pay the account, telling him with great truth, that I had no money; but that if his bill were reduced one half I would give him a draft on Alexandria which would be cashed in the Havannah, provided he procured me a substantial suit of clothes, linen, boots, and so forth for Charles and myself. I was exceedingly anxious to draw such a check upon your agents in Alexandria, as I thought it the only possible way to advise you of my existence and whereabouts. At first he refused to abate a tittle of his bill, but finally consented when I agreed to pay five hundred Mexican dollars for the outfit for myself and servant. Charles had spread exaggerated reports of my wealth through the community by means of the priest, who from the most benevolent reasons determined to relieve us from captivity; and a Jew by the name of Paul Levi,

"'A hungry lean-faced villain,'"

who agreed to furnish us the outfit upon the sum being included in the gaoler's order. A bargain was thus struck, and we were soon comfortably clothed for the first time in many months. Projects and hopes of a new kind now began to intrude themselves on my thoughts, and I conceived a design to affect an escape and mentioned it to Charles, who was roused into new life by the prospect. After many conversations we determined to consult Annetta. Of course she became our accomplice, so ardent is the flame of liberty in every breast, such is the detestation of every human being to slavery. After a consultation conducted, as to Annetta, hurriedly, and from time to time, as she found opportunity to speak to us, when fetching our supplies of food, upon the *quo modo* of our escape, it was determined, if possible, to gain the co-operation of the Jew. Annetta was instructed to offer him a bribe of £500 to furnish us three good horses, a pair of pistols and the tools necessary to break from prison. After much discussion and delay Levi was secured. My heart beat high with hope, and I began to flatter myself that the day was not distant when we should bid our tyrants adieu. To prevent suspicion, Levi purchased our horses at once, pretending they were for a journey he would soon take into the Southern country. I did not afterwards regret the delay of two weeks, which now occurred, as my strength daily increased. Annetta was made acquainted with the spot where these animals were kept, constantly ready against such time as we might effect our escape. It was near the Jew's house, but far enough to enable him to hatch a plausible lie to the effect that they were stolen after we left. Annetta now brought us from the Jew some tools for breaking out, and we went to work nightly. With incredible danger, difficulty, and labour, we made way through the solid wall, cutting through a four inch oak plank. This brought us into the prison yard, but until we could mature a plan for passing the sentinels, we allowed the outer row of stone and its covering of plaster to remain intact. The principal part of this work was done by Charles, while I kept guard at the door to prevent detection. When, however, he was exhausted and took his turn at the door, I worked with all my strength and will, and greatly to his admiration. He often said 'I hab no ideum Massa Peyton hab sich slight ob hand, sich strength—white man hard to beat.' While this work was occupying us, both our health and spirits improved, and I often thought of your remark, 'that the busiest and most laborious are generally the happiest and most successful.'

"As a Monsieur Blicq leaves here to-day, for Detroit, intending to travel thence to New York, I entrust this to him to be there posted. You will thus be relieved of all anxiety as to myself, and will understand the cause of my drafts upon your agents in Alexandria, should they be presented for payment before my return. I am exceedingly anxious to proceed upon my homeward journey, and am only detained by the necessity of recruiting my health before I set forth again. I shall proceed hence this day week, and make my way through the new settlements in Kentucky to Western Virginia and thence by the Greenbrier to Staunton and Charlottesville.

"If the Howes have returned to Virginia, I hope you will immediately make their acquaintance and give them my kind regards and remembrances, and a brief account of my adventures since I had the pleasure to meet them in Jamaica.

"It may be proper for me to say here that the attachment which I formed in Jamaica for Miss Howe has increased in strength and intensity, notwithstanding our separation, and I am satisfied is based upon genuine affection. I did not know so much when in that lovely island, where the very air breathes nothing but transport and delight, nor did I believe so much—I rather attributed my feelings to the warmth of my temper and the ardent sensibility of my mind. To have met a young countrywoman in that distant corner of the world must, under any circumstances, have filled me with joy, but when she was exceedingly pretty, highly accomplished, and captivating in the extreme, it is not to be wondered at that the syren enticed me unconsciously into her snares. She expressed her satisfaction at meeting with a Virginian so very unexpectedly, and to a considerable extent reserve was thrown off on both sides. Expecting, however, to see her in the spring, I steeled my heart by timely reflection against premature advances. However interesting our conversations, none of them were confidential or upon the immediate subject of love. I have been subsequently racked by torture, when reflecting over my coolness and reserve on these occasions. On my neglect to declare my passion, from an apprehension that it might be a mere temporary ebullition, and that I might be repulsed, lest this neglect to seize a golden opportunity may not have deprived me for ever of the society of the most incomparable woman in the world. I must beg you, therefore, my dear father, as you value my happiness, to advise Miss Howe's family somewhat of my feelings."

CHAPTER IX.

MR. HOWE VISITS ENGLAND IN PURSUIT OF LEGAL BUSINESS.—SECURES A GREAT SUCCESS.—FORMS THE ACQUAINTANCE OF AN AMICUS CURIA.—JIMMY JONES.—RETURNS TO JAMAICA TO FIND HIS WIFE FURIOUS AND HIS DAUGHTER IN LOVE.—THE FAMILY AT HOME ON THE OCCOQUAN IN VIRGINIA.

As the Howe family subsequently become mixed up in the affairs of my grandfather playing a more or less interesting part in the *mélange* according to the taste of the reader, he will not probably object if we pause for a moment, to introduce them more fully to his knowledge.

While the events as related in the last chapter were transpiring, Mr. Howe, father of the fair enchantress, who had so rapidly excited the enthusiasm, and gained the affections of the young Virginian, was busily occupied with legal affairs in England. For many years previous to crossing the Atlantic, Mr. Howe had prosecuted a law suit in London for the recovery of an estate, which his legal advisers in the purlieus of the Temple, assured him was the rightful property of himself, as the eldest surviving representative of the late Grubham Howe, Esq., of Cold Barwick, in the county of Wiltshire. For ten years he had followed this matter with no further result than to see his ten successive crops of tobacco swallowed up by the costs, which included exorbitant fees to the rapacious legal reptile, who championed his cause. Worn out by the law's delay and expenses, he determined to visit our old home, (as England is affectionately styled by the cultivated people of Virginia) hoping to find a solution of this wasting controversy. Availing himself of the period when his wife and daughter must visit Jamaica, he accompanied them to that island, and after seeing them comfortably established in their temporary home, proceeded to England, where he arrived late in the autumn of 1772.

Much to his gratification he found on his arrival, that his case, after innumerable difficulties and delays, was at last about to be tried. Establishing himself in the neighbourhood of Westminster, he determined, notwithstanding the numerous calls upon his time, to watch the progress of his suit with the closest scrutiny. Fortunately the matter now required little pushing. The pleadings were completed, the testimony taken, the depositions filed, and the case set down for trial at the next term.

At the term of the Court, which was held according to custom at Westminster, within a few weeks of his arrival, the cause of Howe *v.* Howe came on to be heard. The ablest counsel were employed on either side, and the case was argued at great length, with zeal, earnestness, and ability, and an amount of legal learning perfectly astonishing to the Virginian planter. Day after day he attended the Hall of justice with paper and pencil, taking notes of the salient points and making comments upon the forensic arguments of his own and the opposing counsel. At the end of which time he declared that, whereas when he left Virginia he understood something of the matter at issue; but now, so many were the new points raised, and so entangled had the case become under professional manipulation, so buried in a mass of legal learning, that he was completely bewildered and totally at fault how to determine which was the better cause. Not so his counsel, who cried "bravo!" and pronounced the progress of the case all that could be desired.

A fortnight was consumed over this important cause, and the learned judges were finally considering of their judgment. The impression made upon the minds of the barristers who had been unengaged, and were, therefore, impartial spectators, was now very freely expressed, and was to the effect that Mr. Howe had no just cause of action, no conclusive testimony in his behalf, and, consequently, no prospect of success—not the slightest shadow of a chance: that his case, in a word, so far from having been made out, had utterly failed; that he and his family were neither entitled by law nor equity to the property in dispute, nor any part of it, but that it belonged either to the present occcupiers, or in default of their title, to a branch of the family which had emigrated some years previous to Cape Colony, and were supposed, or, at least, were reported to be, extinct.

One of Mr. Howe's court friends had, at an early day, informed him that, in his opinion, he, Mr. Howe, had no prospect whatever of success. This friend, commonly called Mr. Jimmy Jones—his real name was James Scroggin Jones—was one of those persons of singular taste and habits, who attend the courts as spectators, at every term, through years, with the punctuality and regularity of the bench and the bar, a man who had thus acquired a vast fund of confused and disjointed legal knowledge, impossible however to be applied. Mr. Jones, who was now much in Mr. Howe's company, going often, on the invitation of the Virginian, to partake of his quiet dinner and bottle of crusty port, as well as to talk over the matter "*in re*" while blowing a comfortable cloud, informed him, almost with tears in his eyes, for he had acquired a fraternal affection for Mr. Howe, that his case was hopeless.

"So bad a show 'ave you made of it," said Mr. Jones, upon the evening the case closed, "that no 'ope is left you, my friend, even in that fruitful source of 'ope with hall litigants, the glorious uncertainty of the law."

"I fully believe you," said the planter, "I once had hope when reading my lawyer's sanguine letters in Virginia. Since I have heard the argument, that hope is lost. I am lost—my head's gone—such a jumble, such a muddle have the legal cooks made of the broth! I am sure if they understand the case, what it depends upon, where the gist of it lies, it is more than any unprofessional human being can conscientiously declare."

"I beg your pardon," said Mr. Jimmy Jones, " it is very simple, if you will honly look hat it disinterestedly."

"But how can I?" broke in the unfortunate planter. "Have I not lost ten crops of tobacco in the expenses, and more besides. Have I not been buoyed up with false and delusive hopes for years—for years been harassed with doubts, weighed down with anxinty and care, and been led even to crossing the Atlantic to look after this affair, and now you talk to me of being disinterested ?"

"'Old, be calm, my worthy friend," said Mr. Jones, "you misunderstand my drift. I only mean if you look hat the matter in a purely legal and equitable point of view, you must see that your counsel has been mistaken from the commencement, and has hintentionally or hinnocently, as the case may be, led you into herror. It pains me deeply, but I must prevent your hentertaining false 'opes, it is not your branch, but the 'Owes of South Africa who hare entitled to the property, if those in England hare not."

With a heavy groan, the disappointed planter ejaculated, "I fear it must be so."

The evening wore away in this kind of desultory conversation, Mr. Jones endeavouring from time to time to administer some consolation to him, but in vain. Next morning the planter's chagrin was heightened by learning from several solicitors whose acquaintance he had made pending the suit, gentlemen of acknowledged learning, experience and ability, that his cause was hopeless.

During the whole of the day he sauntered through the West-end parks, endeavouring to walk off the effects of his disappointment and ruminating upon his family and home in dear old Virginia, which he cursed himself a thousand times for having abandoned in the wretched greed of gain.

"Let me once get back and I'll defy the world to make me leave again!" he cried so loudly as he paced Rotten Row, in gloomy abstraction that he caused the horse of an equestrian to bolt, and was thought by the loungers in that fashionable haunt to be a dangerous madman at large.

On returning in the evening to his lodgings, he heard from the pertinacious Mr. Jones, who would not even go to the parks to scent the breezes during term time that the Chief Justice had announced that their decision in the case of Howe *v.* Howe would be pronounced on the following morning.

Early the next day the court was crowded to excess. Howe *v.* Howe was a *cause célèbre*, a vast amount of property depended upon it, the friends, relatives, and, for all that, the enemies, of both parties were assembled. In due season the court opened, and "my Lord" proceeded at learned length to pronounce the decision of two of the judges in favour of the claim of the Virginian, on every point and in every particular. Intense excitement, but a restrained silence, followed this announcement. Those legal gentlemen who had advised Mr. Howe of his want of action stood confounded—seemed stunned—his friend Mr. Jones was overcome with unexpected joy, and retired to the lobby for fresh air. His Lordship hurriedly recapitulated the opinions of the dissenting judges, who pronounced against the claim of Mr. Howe as decidedly as the others pronounced in his favour. Here was a muddle, a lock, a legal knot. While people were thinking what will be done —the knot was severed. A judge was withdrawn. Happy expedient! And this left the decision in favour of the plaintiff. Mr. Howe had gained. Jimmy Jones was in the act of cheering when he was silenced by his Lordship, who gave the defendant against the next term to take an appeal, and, until then, ordered all matters of costs to remain in abeyance, suspended. Here was a "hitch" at the pinch of the hill, and Mr. Jones gave over his cheer to ruminate upon "the point."

As may be imagined, Mr. Howe returned to his lodgings in a somewhat different frame of mind from that in which he left them in the morning. Soon he was overwhelmed with visits from the friends, counsel, attorneys and legal retainers of the other side. These sought, from day to day, to arouse his fears by speaking largely of the appeal, and of the stupendous costs which it would entail upon him and the certainty of their success. After a vast amount of this kind of manœuvering a distinct proposition for compromise came from the opposite side. Mr. Howe's legal adviser, who delighted in the fray and spoils of battle, protested against such a pitiful termination of the proceedings. The Virginian, however, was sufficiently amused, after twelve years, with the "forensic fight," and listened with favourable ears to these propositions, and, to make a long story short, the contested case was finally compromised by Mr. Howe's receiving the estimated value of the ten crops of tobacco expended in the litigation, his entire costs, and the round sum of £36,000, The defendant was thus left with the landed property, and the mesne profits.

This successful termination of a "most harassing business" as the Virginian planter afterwards complacently termed it, left him free to make his preparations to rejoin his family in the West Indies Divesting himself immediately of the large sum received on the compromise, he placed the whole in the 3 per cents. for the sole use and benefit of his only daughter. Having no other children, he afterwards declared that he sunk the money in the funds as well to provide a certain support for his daughter Annie, as to rid himself of all trouble in connection with it. His estates in Virginia gave him quite enough trouble of themselves. He was closely occupied with these matters and in making purchases for the use of his colonial estates, when he received a letter from his wife, from which we make the following extract. It gave him the first intelligence of my grandfather's arrival in the Antilles.

From Mrs. Howe's letter of September, 1773.

"I must not neglect to inform you that we have had for some weeks past a pleasant addition to our society, in the son of Mr. John Peyton, of Stoney Hill. The young gentleman came out to adjust some important affairs for his father, which I hear he has successfully concluded. He is highly cultivated and most amiable, is easy, civil, and respectful in his behaviour, is what may be termed a gentleman of thorough good breeding. I have felt less solitary and more contented since his arrival, and have had with him many agreeable conversations about Virginia and our friends there, with numbers of whom he is acquainted. He returns within a few days to Virginia, and has promised to make a visit to Belleville immediately upon our arrival. This I do not doubt he will do, for, with all his partialities for my society, I think he prefers that of our dear Annie. I must not neglect to say that he carries what Lord Bacon styles 'a perpetual letter of recommendation,' a pleasing figure, being of comely presence and engaging manners."

Having finally arranged his affairs, Mr. Howe sailed for the West Indies, having in company Mr. Jimmy Jones. During the progress of his vexatious but successfully terminated suit and their long evening conferences upon knotty points of law, a warm friendship sprung up between them, and when Mr. Howe was about to take his departure. Mr. Jones expressed a wish to accompany him. The Virginian was delighted and the matter was soon arranged. Mr. Jones informed him that he was alone in the world, had neither business nor cares, in other words, no family or friends, and had fallen into the inveterate habit of attending the courts from having nothing to occupy his time. That he was fond of fishing as much so as of the law, and would find ample amusement to fill up his time throwing a line in the Occoquan.

"Then, my dear sir," said Mr. Howe, "go with me to Belleville and make it your home. You're the best company in the world, and will have it all your own way among our colonial lawyers. Nothing will make me happier, my dear Jones. We will live and die together in old Virginny."

So the matter was arranged, and Mr. Jimmy Jones for the first time in his life had something to do, preparing for the voyage, and for the first time in thirty years was missed from the benches of the law court. The two gentlemen left England in December, and arrived in Jamaica in the month of February 1774.

Mr. Howe was much concerned to find that though his daughter's health was greatly improved, she seemed a prey to melancholy. Little, however, did he divine the cause, for—

> "She never told her love,
> But let concealment, like a worm i' the bud;
> Feed on her damask cheek."

It may be easily imagined that a noble and gallant spirit like that of the young Virginian could not be long in the society of a susceptible lady, without making an impression upon her heart. Such was the case. Annie Howe, with a quick perception of true nobility of character, had silently observed the handsome and accomplished Virginian during his stay in Spanish Town, and her love for him was a secret, "the only jewel of her speechless thought." How strange is the birth, how quick is the growth of this mysterious passion!

Mr. Howe communicated, for the first time, to his wife, his disposition of the £36,000 received on compromising the law suit. He heard from his wife, too, more of the young gentleman, to whom she alluded, in the extract taken from her letter the previous autumn, and what she supposed was his heartless conduct

After paying marked attention to Annie during his visit, thereby creating the deepest interest in himself on her part, and giving rise to no small amount of gossip in the community, ill-natured people saying "if they were not engaged they ought to be," and so forth; after having almost told his love, but still refrained from doing so, and making no formal offer of his hand, but leaving the impression upon the poor girl's mind that he would keep up a correspondence till their return to Virginia, he had gone off to New Orleans, the wicked creature! and they had not heard of him since.

"The duplicity and cruelty of some men is above comprehension," said the excited lady. "And to think of such blackness of heart, such refinement of cruelty, such desperate wickedness under cover of those blue eyes, that frank countenance, and those flaxen locks! Sir," cried she to her listening husband, "never believe in appearances, nothing is more deceitful."

"But," said Mr. Howe, "may there not be some explanation of this disagreeable business consistent with the young man's honour?"

"No, sir; none!" said his wife. "We know he arrived in New Orleans from this note, (holding up a letter) in which he seems to laugh at us, and he must have arrived in Virginia months and months ago. There can be no explanation of his conduct. I wish to hear none. No——"

She stopped here to recover her breath, a pause which the phlegmatical husband embraced to cast his eyes over the following epistle, to which his wife referred as " this note."

"New Orleans.

"My Dear Mrs. Howe,

"I have only a moment to write to announce my arrival here. There are few opportunities of sending letters directly to Jamaica, and I avail myself of the present, the more eagerly, to thank you for all the kindness and hospitality extended to me by yourself and family during my recent visit to the island. I shall always treasure the recollection of it with the greatest sensibility, and shall never cease to felicitate myself upon my good luck in meeting yourself and Miss Howe. My sojourn here will be brief, when I proceed to St. Augustine, from whence I shall post to Miss Howe a copy of my diary since leaving Jamaica, brought down to that date. She flattered me by asking me to give her some account of the remarkable places I am visiting, on my return to Virginia. I trust she will pardon the liberty I shall take in anticipating that time, by sending to Jamaica some excerpts from my note book. They will probably serve to amuse her during the approaching winter season, if such a thing as winter exists in your sunny isle.

"Make my respectful compliments to Miss Howe, and with many, many wishes for her entire restoration to health, and many anticipations of the great pleasure it will give me to renew my friendship with her and yourself in the spring.

"I am, believe me, dear Mrs. Howe,
"Faithfully your friend,
"J. R. PEYTON."

When the worthy planter finished the perusal of this epistle, he was impressed with the sincere and straightforward character of the writer and so said to his wife.

"You may rest sure of one thing," said he, "there are good reasons for not hearing from him, suspend your judgment, at least until something further is known. I am ignorant certainly of the young man's character, though I am pleased with the way in which he writes, but if he be a chip of the old block—I know his father's character well—ugly as the matter now looks, it will come right in the end. Courage!"

At this juncture Mr. Jimmy Jones entered the room, and, as he now stood in the position of a friend of the family, was made acquainted with the domestic trouble, and consulted on the subject.

"My dear madam, from what you tell me of the young man, I take the impression," said Mr. Jones, "that he is a gay deceiver, a 'eartless villain. What we call in London a box-lobby lounger, one of your hupstart cubs who spend the best part of the day in Pall Mall, St. James' and Bond Streets; who, without any parts, fancy themselves fine fellows, and strive by loose morals to acquire a reputation for gallantry, and who hassume fierce airs to conceal their want of spirit. Bucks who will ruin an innocent girl, but take very good care never to endanger their carcases by meddling with villanous saltpetre nor cold iron. There may be characters more wicked, though I doubt it; certainly there are none more contemptible. My friend Mr. Howe is of too easy a nature."

"Come, come, Jimmy," said Mr. Howe, "don't make an ass of yourself. I know our people better than you. I have a presentiment it will all end well." Turning to his wife he said:—

"Comfort, dear mother, God is much displeased
That you take with unthankfulness his doing."

On occasions Mr. Howe was a stern imperious man, notwithstanding his amiable temper, and his manner now forbade another word from wife or friend. Mr. Jones rubbed his hands, smiled, and was silent. Mrs. Howe left the room in tears.

Two months after this conversation in Jamaica, Mr. Howe and his family, which included Mr. Jimmy Jones, were re-established in their old quarters at Belleville, in Virginia. The news was now rife in the neighbourhood of the loss of their young countyman Peyton. No one could explain his absence, the family at "Stoney Hall" were plunged in the depths of grief, though kind friends sought to sustain their spirits, to keep alive their hopes by suggesting every sanguine view of the situation. Everything, however, connected with his fate was left in painful suspense. To the Howes there was one, and but one pleasant feature in the case; Mrs. Howe and Jimmy Jones had grossly wronged and defamed the character of the missing gentleman. This was now clear as the noonday sun. The good lady endeavoured to make amends for what she had previously said, and was now as indiscreetly lavish in her encomiums on my grandfather as she had before been in her censures.

> "The indiscreet with blind aversion run
> Into one fault, when they another shun."

Pale was the visage, and quick came and went the breath of the unhappy girl whose soul sickened at these praises of one whom she loved, and of whose society she feared death had for ever robbed her.

CHAPTER X.

ABSENT BUT NOT FORGOTTEN.—A RIVAL IN THE FIELD.—CAPTAIN PELHAM IN A NEW CHARACTER.

THIS history would be incomplete were it not mentioned that in the society of Jamaica there was no more general favourite with the fair sex than Captain Pelham, R.E., who had accompanied my grandfather on his first excursion across the island. Captain Pelham was the younger son of an ancient English family which had fallen into moderate circumstances, or "decay," as it was sarcastically termed, since they were under the necessity of gaining a livelihood by the "sweat of the brow." He was six feet two inches high, of pleasing countenance, good manners, and excellent sense. Full of life and spirit, he entered the military service determined to hew his way to fortune. Whatever justification there may have been in the depleted exchequer of his family for applying to them the word "decay," there were no signs or symptoms of feebleness or decline about the young lieutenant's physique. He was indeed a young giant, mettlesome, and full of pluck and spirit. Possessing nothing beyond his pay and an occasional fifty pound note, presented by a maiden gentlewoman, an aunt residing in Dorset, he early made up his mind to steer clear of matrimonial alliances, at least, as he said, in the days of his *juvenescence*. This was a luxury with which he hoped to crown his honours as a general officer. In vain, therefore, was it that managing mamas and sentimental and romantic young ladies conspired against his liberty and peace of mind. He was not to be so "done for." He was, of course, at every party, ball, pic-nic, or other social gathering, because he considered it part of his duty to contribute his share to the amusement of society; besides, he was fond of dancing, and, in a general way was not averse to the society of pretty young ladies. On the contrary, so far from it, he delighted to be in their company. The failure of the belles, however, to captivate the gallant officer gave rise to much comment. Mothers said he was a heartless fortune hunter, the girls said he had no soul, no sympathy, was dead to gentle and generous emotions. Sensible and disinterested people knew it was because, having scarcely enough to keep soul and body together, he shrank from assuming the responsibility of a wife and family.

Notwithstanding, however, the unfavourable light in which he was professedly viewed by ladies, old and young, he was always welcomed by them, and the young damsels relaxed none of their seductive arts in a continued effort to entrap his heart. Between the strategy of the mothers, and their skill was Napoleonic, and the graces of the daughters, and these were really pretty and engaging girls, not without certain tactics, Pelham was like a strong fortress closely besieged. He bore himself, however, like a hero, showed no signs of weakness, gave no symptoms of capitulation to the enemies forces. Affairs proceeded thus till both old and young ladies began to despair of securing the Pelham alliance, though it had been lisped by many a promising young tactician, when it was thought it would be reported to him, that "no one knew how economical she could be, on how little she could live. It was all a mistake supposing young ladies extravagant, that they required anything considerable on which to dress; that, for herself, whatever might be the case with other girls, she was not fond of silks and jewels, and could live and love in a cottage. Aye, and would prefer it, to love in the most sumptuous palace. The simple idea was enchanting."

The gallant lieutenant heard all this, and was still inflexible. Conscious that he required daily so much beef and pudding, so much brandy and soda, so much tobacco and so many cigars, for personal comfort and consumption; he strongly suspected, after the knot matrimonial was tied, his lovely Juliana would demand for her peculiar feminine wants a similar supply. Yes, this young man resolutely resisted every appeal made to his understanding and to his heart, went to parties and indulged in the dance made fashionable calls, and took the ladies on pleasure excursions. Sent them flowers with his compliments, assisted them at the street crossings, sang for them at soirées, presented them with books, walked with them through the lanes, and risked his life on the cliffs to assist and amuse them, and when the day was over, racked his burning brain writing verses to their "eye-brows," and yet the insensible, obdurate, unprincipled fellow would not go a step further (as said the general feminine voice, he was in honour bound after his attentions) and make one of them his wife. Flinty and cruel-hearted wretch, were some of the numerous choice epithets now lavished upon poor Pelham. One spinster, Edith Splutter, said he had been long enough in the Island, it was time he was going; another wished he had already gone; some that they had never seen him. One hysterical young lady of thirty-six, declared he had forced her to fall in love with him, by practising his seductive arts of fascination; that he was a refined villain, and merely charmed her to amuse himself; that now he was gay and light-hearted, while she was in a rapid decline—a galloping consumption. Should never recover! no, never!

While the young officer was thus defying all attacks, standing out like a grey old fortress against every assault, and frowning from its heights upon the enemies below, a foe stole within the citadel, and sapped the foundations of its strength. The indifferent young gentleman who had so long defied the arts of love, suddenly re-appeared after his visit to Spanish Town, with a lean cheek, sunken eye, and neglected beard! His gay companions in the Titchfield Fort could scarcely credit the evidences of their senses. What change had come o'er the spirit of his dream, that the gallant Pelham should wander about, "his hose ungartered, his bonnet unbanded, his sleeve unbuttoned, his shoe untied, and everything about him demonstrating a careless desolation?"

The truth is, on his journey he had fallen in love! No one among the numerous admirers of Annie Howe in Jamaica felt for her a deeper, purer admiration and affection than the young officer. He had succumbed to her charms on first sight; the longer he knew her, the more he loved her. He thought, however, that 'My Grandfather' (they both made her acquaintance at the same time), was pleased with her, and that she gave some —the faintest possible kind of preference—for his society. Consequently, he hesitated to say to her a word of the tumultuous feelings which raged within his breast. When, however, his Virginian friend sailed for New Orleans without making any special advance to Miss Howe, or alluding to her in conversation with him, feeling for her only, as Pelham thought, the admiration and affection of a friend, he could no longer restrain his feelings; forgot all his prudence, and determined to make an avowal of his love. He accordingly commenced his preparations to return to the southern side of the island as the first land breeze was bellying the sails of the vessel which bore his Virginian friend to "other shores." Never before had the gallant fellow been entangled by the silken cords and flowery chains of love. His fancy had not been allured, nor his tastes effeminated by the softness of pleasure. He was a bold, hardy, handsome soldier, of masculine mind, superior to low sensual enjoyments and vulgar voluptuousness. He arrived in Spanish Town as if he travelled with the wind for his companion, and the tempest for his comrade. He rode across the highest peaks and the deepest cock-pits of Jamaica, with the reckless speed of John Gilpin. Arrived, he rested a day to compose his nerves, and then with his previous impatience and impetuosity sought the presence of Annie Howe, and declared his love with passionate warmth. There was no wooing, no diplomacy—nothing but the ardour, the unthinking enthusiasm of the soldier. Of course, the gallant knight was unhorsed, prostrated in the dust, repulsed, defeated.

"Annie! oh! dear Annie!" he exclaimed.

But hold! We must not withdraw the curtain which covers this painful episode in the lives of two noble creatures.

To make a long story short, Captain Pelham, finding all hope of success vain and futile, at least for the present, returned to Tichfield. He now travelled at a snail's pace: his head hung down, his eyes upon the ground. "Like a wounded snake, he drew his slow length along." He was not, however, in despair. It gave him inexpressible happiness to know that while Annie Howe did not love him, she was not the affianced of another. This single ray of sunshine kept up daylight in his heart. She might still be won. He would make the effort. By constancy, by every act of devotion, by demonstrating his sincerity, he might succeed. Clinging to this hope, he kept up his acquaintance with the family, making repeated visits to Tichfield, though he received not the slightest encouragement from Annie Howe. Mrs. Howe, who was under the impression that my grandfather had trifled with the affections of her daughter, encouraged Captain Pelham, and endeavoured to create an interest on his behalf in the mind of her daughter, hoping thus to divert her attention from the absorbing subject of her first love. Affairs were in this condition when Mr. Howe returned from England with his legal friend, Mr. Jimmy Jones. That gentleman, as we have seen in the previous chapter, took a different view of affairs from his wife, and all encouragement from Mrs. Howe to young Pelham was discontinued. When bidding him adieu, on their return to Virginia, Annie Howe, and indeed, the family said, if Captain Pelham should ever carry out his purpose of visiting Virginia, it would give them much pleasure to see him, as a friend, at Belleville. Annie Howe closed the door to hope, by saying to him when alone, "I can never see you, save as a friend."

CHAPTER XI.

HE RESUMES HIS LETTER FROM ST. LOUIS.—HIS ESCAPE FROM THE SANTA FE PRISON AND FLIGHT ACROSS THE ROCKY MOUNTAINS.—TRAVERSES THE GREAT PLAINS OF THE INTERIOR OF NORTH AMERICA AND ARRIVES IN ST. LOUIS GUIDED BY AN OSAGE WARRIOR.

"Having provided a means of escape from our cell, we were now to consider a plan for passing the sentinels, who constantly kept guard over the outer gate. While weighing first one plan and then another, we were informed by Annetta that her parents would attend the wedding of a young friend on the 10th of March. On that night no one would be on the premises but herself, and two young brothers and the sentinels. Charles immediately proposed that we should enter the court-yard through the opening in the prison wall on that occasion, and take our chance of escape by falling upon and murdering the guard. This plan, however, being too uncertain of execution, and sure from the noise it would create to call forth the rest of the guard, and alarm the town. I dismissed it as not feasible. I had now become wonderfully prudent, for I saw that it was a crisis of more importance than any other of my life—a crisis in which haste, or too much delay, irresolution, or yielding to the ill-considered expedient of Charles, would be fatal. Having dismissed his proposition, it was suggested by Annetta that she should poison the sentinels in a cup of hot coffee, which she said they would be glad to get about midnight, especially as the weather was now quite cold. Charles was delighted with this proposition, and strongly urged me to agree to it. Upon reflection I rejected this scheme also, and suggested that instead of poisoning the sentinels, Annetta should content herself with drugging them, by putting laudanum in their coffee. This, I imagined, would answer our purposes equally well, and preserve us from the stain of blood. Both were enraptured at my proposition, accordingly it was immediately determined upon, and Annetta instructed to prepare for its execution. Next day she obtained the opiate through the Jew, who pretended that it was to drench a sick horse. She was further directed to provide some jerked beef, a few bottles of spirits, and to advise the Jew of the night upon which we expected to escape. She executed every commission with which she was entrusted with prudence, and a skill beyond her years. When, since thinking of the discretion she displayed in these delicate matters, my mind has recurred to the words of Prospero, who says of Miranda—

"'—— She will outstrip all praise,
And make it halt behind her.'

The wedding night arrived, and luckily for the execution of our enterprise, we heard the ceremony of marriage was to be followed by a dance or fandango, as the Spaniards call it. The night was dark, and we awaited with breathless impatience the hour when the jailor and his wife would depart. As the clock struck eight, the turnkey made his usual circuit of the wards. He then informed the sentinels, since there was no occasion to open the cells during his absence, the prisoners having received their evening supply of bread and water, he should retain the keys in his custody. Annetta, however, said the turnkey, would remain in charge of his apartment, and in case his presence was required, he directed that she might be despatched to him at the fandango. With this the jailor, whose name was Ximenes, and who was as tyrannical, cruel, and infamous a villain as ever disgraced human nature, a wretch who could smile and murder whilst he smiled, sallied forth with his wife, who was his worthy companion in meanness and cruelty. It was now nearly nine o'clock, and Annetta came to our cell to whisper that all was ready; that she had provided provisions, spirits, &c., and only wished to know the least suspicious way to offer the sentinels coffee. While talking, one of these fellows advancing, asked in a loud voice—

"'What are you doing here?'

"*Annetta:* 'I was merely looking at these poor prisoners and wondering how long they could live under such cruel treatment.'

"*Sentinel:* 'That's none of your business. They are French pirates, and had they met their deserts would have been hang longed ago. They are the worst kind of pirates, they wish to steal our land, to upset our authority, and to make themselves masters of this country, eh! my boys, (leering at us,) you've undertaken 'a big job.'"

"By this time the second sentinel arrived on the spot and inquired,

"'What's up among ye?'

"'Oh,' said Annetta, 'I was merely asking these poor fellows, as this was a wedding night, whether they would not like to have a cup of hot coffee and a piece of sweet-bread, do permit me to give it them for the sake of our Redeemer.'

"'You little rogue,' said the sentinel, 'are you siding with our enemies?'

"'Naughty man,' said Annetta, 'don't talk that way, what harm have the poor fellows done us. They are our brother human beings, let us for the love of the Holy Virgin sooth their misery for a moment, by a little supper. If you will let me give them some, each of you shall have a cup of coffee, a nice roll and a glass of rum to boot.'

"'Good, it's a bargain,' said the sentinels, 'be in a

hurry, my pretty one, get it ready, and let both coffee and rum be strong.'

"Annetta disappeared, and in a half hour brought us coffee, having upon the same platter two cups heavily drugged for the guard. These fellows no sooner snuffed the delicious aroma of the fragrant berry than they advanced and helping themselves to a buttered roll, quickly gulped down, both roll and coffee. Not satisfied, they asked for more, which Annetta quickly brought, after having drugged the second cup as heavily as the first. The lazy sentinels then returned to their post, saying pray don't forget the rum.

"'Remember,' said one, 'you promised rum and strong to boot.'

"About five minutes after, one called—

"'Annetta, hurry with that rum, our supper has made us drowsy. Some rum to wake us up.'

"'Yes, Signors, ready in a moment,' said Annetta advancing with two glasses of drugged spirits.

A few moments after this, both sentinels sank upon the ground in lethargic slumbers. In a few minutes the outer covering which had concealed the opening we had made in the prison wall was demolished, and we were in the court. Annetta, who had tied the ribbon of her bonnet under her chin, carried a heavy Spanish cloak and a sack with provisions. Charles took charge of the cloak and sack, and availing ourselves of the condition of the guard, we each appropriated a musket and ammunition from the sleeping enemy—indirectly from the stores of His Majesty the King of Spain—*finis coronat opus.* Thus armed and equipped, we groped our way through the streets, there were no lights in Santa Fé, to the outskirts of the town, and were conducted by Annetta to the Jew's stable. In this building we found Levi on guard, with a dark lanthorn, paper, writing materials, &c. When about to draw him a draft upon Havannah for the £500, he agreed to accept as full compensation for the horses and equipment, and the aid thus far extended to us, he refused to receive the sum, and quick as thought gliding out of the stable, closed the door and turned the key upon us. For an instant we were confounded by this manœuvre, not knowing what it meant, I had only a moment to restrain Charles, who was about to fling himself against the door saying. 'Hold! to all the living there is hope; a living dog is better than a dead lion,' when we heard Levi clearing his villanous throat preparatory to a speech:

"'Now,' said the Jew, speaking from the outside, 'keep quiet, or you will alarm the town, or I will alarm it for you. I have dealt fairly and squarely up to this time, and will do so to the end, only you must be reasonable, and deal fairly and squarely with me. For the great risk I run, for the horses, bridles and saddles, the pistols and food I have provided at great expense of time and money for your use, £500 is no fair equivalent—is not the right figure. Draw the check for a thousand, and hand it through this crevice, and you are at liberty to depart instanter. Refuse compliance, and I shall raise the alarm, and you'll return to prison, and before to-morrow's sun goes down you'll dangle from a tree; make the acquaintance of hemp cord.'

"After a few moments' hurried consultation, seeing the wretch had us 'upon the hip,' I promised to draw the check as he desired. I only asked that he would open the door first and let us prepare to move, and to show that he was honest and willing to confide in us.

"'No, Sir,' said the Jew, with a smiling cheek. 'It is better to do well, than to say well. Time is shortening too, say at once, will you write the check for £1,000 or not?'

"I thought if the mountain will not come to Mahomet, Mahomet must go to the mountain, in other words, no alternative being open to acceptance, I agreed to his extortion, and while writing the check, Charles got the horses ready, as if not doubting the Jew's integrity. Meanwhile Annetta threatened him with the dire vengeance of her family, in case of failure in the issue of our exploit.

"Levi examining my check, and seeing it was in due form, and for £1,000, at sight, and without grace, placed it in the innermost recess of his pocket-book, and opened the door. Ten minutes after I " did void my rheum upon his beard," we were half a mile from the town in a canter, towards the lofty peaks of the Rocky Mountains. Among the articles provided me by the Jew, was a small pocket compass, for which I had specially stipulated. It was by means of this tiny instrument I intended making my way across the Great Western plains, to the mouth of the Pohitenous or Missouri river, which I knew to be in latitude 36° 10′ longitude 90° 5′. Urging our horses on at the top of their speed till morning, we were with the first blushes of Aurora, about forty miles from Santa Fé, in the midst of the Rocky Mountains, perfectly safe from any pursuit or any apprehensions of pursuit.

"Our direction was towards an unexplored region; the roving tribes of savages who inhabited it, were hostile to the Spaniards, and in the depths of winter, few would think of attempting to cross the mountains without a guide or pathway—such were the grounds of our fancied security. Finding at dawn that we were involved in the mountains, we rested four hours, during which we made an excellent breakfast from Annetta's supplies; afterwards tethered the horses on the grassy banks of a stream, and set out on foot in search of a feasible route, across these high and rugged mountains. For three days we were engaged in this arduous undertaking, and finally succeeded; principally through the energy and activity of Charles, who is by the way as active as a kid, and as strong, patient and enduring as a donkey.

"Setting out from our first camping ground on the 9th of February 1774, we made our way to the heights of the mountains, and on the 11th, were at their eastern base. As well as I could form an idea of the height, we were 6,000 feet above the level of the sea, but there was little snow, and what there was lay upon the peaks above us. The air from the west during the day was mild, and during the night, not intensely cold. I attributed this fact to the remarkable mildness of the climate west of the mountains. Only after receding from the mountains travelling N.E., did we experience severe cold. During this time we saw no Indians—at this season they migrate to a softer climate, and better hunting grounds. The abundance of game, however, was truly surprising Among the wild animals is a goat which is very shy, and keeps upon the highest spots. We saw daily the bear, (of a huge size too, are the bears of these regions), the wolf, the bison, elk, deer, beaver, racoon and other species of wild beasts. We were too anxious, however, to get to the plains east of the mountains to take any heed of these. None made any attack upon us; all fled at our approach, such is the terror inspired among the beasts of the field, by the face of him, whom God has given 'dominion over the fish of the sea, the fowl of the air, and over the cattle, and over all the earth, and over every creeping thing that creepeth upon the earth.'

"It was our singular good fortune, too, not to have had up to this time any snow or rain, but we now saw clouds gathering in the sky, and were brought to consider the necessity of providing shelter. I observed also that our provisions were rapidly diminishing, and that there was urgent necessity for a renewal of our supply. I accordingly determined to halt in a cavern which was discovered in the side of the mountain, until such time as we could make provision against these contingencies. The same day (11th of February) we shot two large deer, and, taking off their skins, stretched them upon poles to dry. The 12th and 13th it rained incessantly, but we cared little for this, remaining in the cavern engaged in half-cooking, by a huge wood fire, the venison we were to take on the journey. Annetta was very expert in this operation, and by the evening of the second day we had nearly a hundred pounds of dried and charred meat ready to be packed for future use. The skins of the deer were also 'cured' by the fire, and the two sewed together, making a kind of tent, sufficient to protect us, with our blankets and the Spanish cloak, from rain. We determined, however, the next day, to secure two more bucks, and thus provide ourselves a more commodious tent. During the three days we remained here in these preparations, our horses, who found an ample supply of succulent grass in the ravines and on the banks of the streams, improved in flesh and spirits. On the morning of the 15th we set forth, determined to make, as near as we could guess, thirty miles a-day, and not more, to prevent breaking down the horses, which we estimated would bring us in forty days to St. Louis. We proceeded for twenty-one days without the slightest accident, and without meeting a human being, crossing one great river, which I presumed was the Rio Rouge of Arkansas. We estimated, when we had reached the golden sands of the Rio Rouge that we had made quite one-half of our journey, and could not be more than 600 miles from our destination at this point. Our route had been as near as possible in a straight line, uphill and downhill, following the sinuosities of the country like the Chinese wall. There were few difficulties to be encountered, as the country is generally a level, fertile plain, stretching down from the mountains to the Mississippi. The principal chain of the Rocky Mountains throws out numerous ramifications of greater or less proportions, east and west. In the great water-shed or basin between these mountains and the Mississippi vast quantities of water are accumulated from rain and the melting snow of the mountains, which roll on in mighty rivers to the Gulf. The largest of these rivers is the Missouri, Pohitenous, or mud river, whose course has not been discovered, and the second the one we passed in our journey hither, the Rio Rouge, or Red River, of Arkansas, which is of vast extent, placid and beautiful beyond description, where we saw it.

During these three weeks we slept in our tent comfortably, and subsisted almost entirely upon dried venison, without salt, taking only occasionally at night a gill each of brandy.

"Living after this manner, and riding thirty miles a-day, one would have supposed our strength failing, but on the contrary, I felt my health and vigour constantly improving, and I never saw Charles and Annetta in higher spirits. Our horses were tethered at night near our tent, and large fires kept burning round the spot to frighten off wild beast, who abound to such an extent in this terra incognita, that we passed no night which was not rendered hideous by their screamings and howlings. The weather was now much colder, and I saw indications of an approaching snow storm. I determined, therefore, as our supply of provisions needed to be replenished, to call a halt. This was upon the 10th of March, and as near as I could determine our position, from an old French map, which I carried, we were upon the upper waters of the Missouri. Selecting a well-sheltered spot on the side of a hill covered with trees, we soon excavated, with our bayonets, a kind of chamber in the cliff, the front of which was covered with our deer skins. We were not an hour too soon, for a furious north wind and snow storm set in, and lasted two days, when the ground was covered two feet deep. We were now in a terrible position, for which we had scarcely provided. Our horses almost without food, we feared must perish. Unwilling, however, to part with them till obliged, we turned them loose to seek a subsistance among the shrubs, twigs, and mosses of the forest. The day after the storm subsided, the sun appeared in unclouded majesty. I sallied forth, attended by Charles, in search of game. This we found without stint, many deer and other wild animals having sought shelter in the same skirt of timber with ourselves. This was a great blessing, and we fervently returned thanks to Providence for thus providing us with the means of subsistence. We shot two deer and a young buffalo, the butchering and drying of whose flesh occupied us a week.

During this time we nightly called up our horses, who managed to subsist in the forest. We were delighted, too, to discover about this time a great abatement in the cold. I still thought, however, as we were in a dry spot, with a stock of provisions—such as it was—it was better to continue for the present where we were. We did not move till the 21st of March, when the snow had almost disappeared. Then, setting forth again, we found our horses so enfeebled by their scanty fare, that we could scarcely make twenty miles a day. They were only enabled to do this by reason of the trouble we took to find for them sheltered spots every night on the banks of streams, where there was green grass and young pea vines for their nourishment.

On the 2nd of April, when, as we supposed, about four hundred miles from St. Louis, in attempting to ford a stream, which was much swollen by the melting snow, Annetta's horse was suddenly tripped up and swept away by the current. The courageous girl, who was a good swimmer, rose on the waters like a duck, and after some trouble, was rescued. Charles could render no aid, as he had gone to the opposite shore. Our custom had been for him or myself to first cross a stream, then Annetta, to be followed by the third. Placing Annetta upon my horse, she now passed safely, I holding the while by the horse's mane, and wading or swimming according to the depth of the water. From this point we proceeded on our way, alternately having Annetta behind on the crupper of our horses. We were now following the course of the stream, which I was sure must be a tributary of the Pohitenous. We had also come into a country where there were many Indian settlements, though at long distances. Whenever

The Adventures of my Grandfather. 113

we descried these, we gave them in the language of navigators, "a wide birth." On the 18th of April, we lost a second horse from exhaustion, and surrendering our last to Annetta, continued the journey on foot, till we reached the Pohitenous, on the 28th of April, after a journey of 1,300 miles, as near as we could estimate it. Here the last horse was so completely jaded that we abandoned him, determining to make the residue of the journey as best we could.

"The number of Indians had now so much increased, or rather, we had come so much nearer the towns and villages of those inhabiting the Pohitenous country, that without horses it was impossible to avoid them. Indeed, on horseback, I do not think we could have done so. The next day we entered a village, where we found only old men, women and children. The men had already gone forth to wage war against a tribe known as the Ajoues. The tribe among whom we now found ourselves was the Osage, above them were the Canses and Grandes Eaux tribes. Those over whose territory we had passed, were the Piantias, a wandering tribe, and the Arkansaws. We were hospitably treated by the Osages, and exchanged one of our muskets for a bark canoe, in which I determined to float down the river to St. Louis, and we also procured some provisions consisting of hominy and bison's tongue. I found it not only desirable but indispensable to adopt this plan of reaching St. Louis, as I was now almost helpless from an attack of rheumatism brought on by cold, damp clothes, exposure, and want of suitable nourishment. An old Osage Indian agreed to accompany us to St. Louis for a case of rum, which I was glad to promise him, as his presence would save us from annoyance by the savages. We embarked in our little canoe upon the Pohitenous, which is the most turbid river, I suppose, in the whole world, but by skilful navigation kept clear of all obstacles, and safely arrived here in a fortnight. The land on the river is very fertile, and stretches

I

away in boundless plains, covered in summer with the most luxuriant growth of grass.

"St. Louis, the post where we remain, and of which I must say a word before closing, is, as you know, the capital of Upper Louisiana. It was founded about the year 1763, by a company of fur traders from New Orleans. Thirty-one years before this (in 1732) the French established a colony in Illinois with the ultimate design of uniting, by an extensive line of military posts, Canada and Louisiana. In this year, however, (1763) Louis XV ceded the French North American possessions (or rather the remainder of them) to Spain. It was not till 1768, however, that Upper Louisiana fell into the hands of the Spanish, between four and five years after the tragical events I mentioned in connection with the operations of General the Count O'Reilly at New Orleans. Pardon me for indulging in this historical recital of events with which you are doubtless far more familiar than myself.

"It is situated upon a fine table-land lying high above the Mississippi, originally covered, as much of it still is, with forest. It has received a large accession to its population from French Creole and Illinois emigrants, and is now rapidly becoming a place of importance. It is sixty miles above another settlement called St. Geneviève, which is the only French post on the right bank of the river, until Lower Louisiana, a thousand miles off, is reached. When I leave here, it will be for St. Geneviève, *en route* for the Kentucky settlement."

CHAPTER XII.

THIRD AND LAST LETTER FROM ST. LOUIS.—HE MEETS A VIRGINIAN WHO SUPPLIES HIS WANTS.—MARRIAGE OF HIS VALET WITH ANNETTA XIMENES.—INDIAN HOSTILITIES IN ILLINOIS, INDIANA AND OHIO.—DESCRIPTION OF SANTA FE AND THE PLAINS.

"I HAD scarcely been an hour in St. Louis, before, to my great surprise, I met Mr. Thomas Brent, of Alexandria, who had arrived several days before by way of Detroit, with a party of French fur dealers. He was as much surprised to meet me as I to encounter him; and more so to hear of my adventures since leaving Virginia. From him I have procured a loan to cover my expenses homeward. He has given me much valuable information, which will doubtless be of service on the journey, and one of his St. Louis friends, Mr. Choteaue, will travel part of the way with me.

"The Indians in Ohio are preparing to open hostilities against the whites in Virginia, and he thinks it a hazardous undertaking, that of crossing the country. Everywhere in Ohio the savages are making ready to take up the tomahawk, and he advises me—as the only means of getting forward—to keep south of the Ohio, which I have, from the beginning, thought of doing. On my return, I shall join such forces as Governor Dunmore may raise for a campaign against the Red Skins.

"Shortly after reaching St. Louis, Charles informed me of his wish to marry Annetta. This communication did not surprise me, I suggested, however, that the nuptials might be conveniently postponed till our arrival in Virginia. Both parties, however, seemed so anxious to conclude the affair, that I yielded to their wishes. I am under too many obligations to them to refuse any reasonable request they may make of me. Their conduct throughout the journey convinced me that man is not naturally so debased as our prejudices make him; and when left to its own operations, the human heart is uniformly, kindly, affectionate, and sympathetic. It is only in seasons of trial that the sterling qualities of the human heart are often brought to view, and I frequently feel the truth of Shakspeare's lines, when witnessing the conduct and unerring fidelity of these two persons to each other and to myself—

"'Sweet are the uses of adversity.'

"A French Priest was procured, and the marriage ceremony took place on the evening of the eleventh. Charles and Annetta regarding me, on this interesting occasion, as standing towards them somewhat *in loco parentis*, I gave her away, and after the marriage, requested their attendance in my dining-room, where I proceeded to admonish them after the following parental manner. Such is their youth, inexperience, and ignorance, I thought it indispensable to their happiness that I should give them a little wholesome advice. I may add *par parenthèse*, I should scarcely have had gravity to act my part as *pater familias*, but for the vast fund of experience I have acquired the past year, and the scenes of trial and suffering endured with these two companions of my misfortunes, whom I now regard more in the light of humble friends than as servants.

"In presence of each other, I proceeded substantially as follows :

"I said to Charles, that in order to feel a reasonable hope of being happy in his new condition, he must always look upon his wife as his equal and treat her with kindness, respect and attention: cheerfully comply with all her reasonable demands; consult her upon all matters affecting his interests, as she was more deeply interested than any one else in his success, and never if in trouble or embarrassment to conceal it from her; but to make her the repositorium of his innermost thoughts and feelings.

"To Annetta, I said, 'it was her duty to leave nothing undone to render Charles and his home, (when he got one), happy and to gratefully reciprocate his kindness and attention, and always on his return to receive him with a pleasant smile and happy countenance. That it was her duty to gratify his tastes and inclinations in the management of their domestic affairs, as also in her dress, manners and deportment. Never to attempt to obtain the mastery over or to rule him, as if she succeeded, it would only degrade him and herself. Not only to comply cheerfully with his wishes, but to seek to anticipate them, to avoid all disputations and quarrels, or subjects likely to lead to them, especially in company. Never interfere with his business, still less to attempt to interfere in its management. Never under any circumstances to attempt to speak to friends or acquaintances of the failings or imperfections of her husband, that whatever pledge of secrecy she might exact, if she spoke of such matters, sooner or later they would become subjects of discussion among the neighbouring gossips. That if ill luck attend him, she must be prepared to share his misfortunes, as cheerfully as if lucky she would partake of his fortunes. That unless their union was based upon real and devoted affection, they would find marriage a weary bondage, and the 'silken cords' a grating chain, a chain which passion may have wreathed with roses, but which when passion's roses had withered, would betray the iron links, an iron too that would enter the soul.'

"I concluded by advising them that marriage was the

foundation of one of the most sacred and important institutions in society—that of a family—which was nothing more or less than a little commonwealth, jointly governed by the parents, but more especially by the husband, who was the legal and responsible head of the house. That it imposed upon the father the duty and responsibility of properly rearing his children, of giving them a certain education and trade, or profession by which they would be enabled, at the proper age, to procure a subsistance. Dilating upon these matters at considerable length, I finally dismissed them with the present of a sovereign each to make merry against the 15th instant, when we should leave for Kentucky. They seemed very happy at the conclusion of their marriage ceremony, and not less so at the termination of my half-sermonizing remarks.

"Not wishing to break the continuity of my narrative since leaving New Orleans, by any particular description of the country through which I passed, what I have to say upon this subject is reserved for a paper herewith enclosed."

SOME DESCRIPTIONS OF THE INTERIOR

Enclosed in the preceding letter.

"Of the valley of the Rio de Norte, I shall have little to say. This country has been visited and described by numerous French and Spanish travellers. My brief space must be given to a hurried description of those vast solitudes lying between the Rocky Mountains and the Mississippi. Of the valley of the Rio Grande, I may say briefly I was much pleased with its fertile appearance, and delighted with the serenity of the air. The soil is a sandy-loam, very light, and highly productive.

When irrigated, it produces two crops a year. Yet, notwithstanding the extreme fertility of the soil, the bad administration of government, conspiring with the indolence of the inhabitants, leaves it unpopulous and uncultivated.

Producing corn, wine, oil, fruits, cotton, and all the necessaries of life, under a proper system of agriculture and of laws it would become an earthly paradise.

"Advancing up this valley I saw many horses, mules, oxen, sheep and goats feeding in the open air. These herds constitute the chief source of wealth of the inhabitants; more interesting were several ruins at Quivira, where we remained the night indicating, as they do, a former civilization. I was permitted to make a short examination of them, on promising to pay 5 dollars at Santa Fé, where I hoped to raise a loan. I was informed that they were the ruins of the Aborigines, but I do not think so. The slight view I had of them was enough to convince me that they were of Spanish origin. On the journey we suffered greatly from the heat, which was sometimes in the day, 100° F. in the sun. The temperature of this province varies, however, with the latitude and the nature and height of the table-lands.

"As I approached the post of Santa Fé, I was struck with a mixed sensation of surprise and delight at its appearance. The first view is really enchanting. It is situated upon the slopes of hills, and the green fields and luxuriant foliage in which it is embosomed, even at the advanced season of our arrival, gave it a most lovely and picturesque aspect. The surrounding meadows, which are green and beautiful, even in winter, are ornamented with many magnificent flowers, crimson, scarlet, white, pink, and purple. A nearer approach to the town destroyed the charming vision, the houses are low and inferior, constructed of *adaube*, (bricks dried in the sun), the streets filthy and loathsome, and the population indolent and indifferent, a miserable lot of emaciated, sun-burnt and dejected-looking Spaniards. Though a place of inconsiderable size, Santa Fé has been laid out on a grand scale. I have said enough of our imprisonment there to give you every assurance of the sincere pleasure with which we turned our backs upon it, to enter the wild, solitary, and unexplored regions, which separate the Rocky Mountains from the Mississippi. This region is so vast that a description of it is no easy matter. I shall only give you a sketch of its general characteristics, and a few details concerning those striking points which came under my observation, and which modify those characteristics. This country is watered by many streams, such as the Canadian, the Rio Rouge, the White, the Cansas, the Arkansas, the Niobrarah, the Keha-Pahah, the Pohitenous, and other rivers, whose names, if they have any, are unknown to civilized man. The whole is a vast plain stretching down from the lofty summits of the Rocky Mountains to the Mississippi, and until the traveller arrives within three hundred miles of the river, is devoid of trees, except on the borders of rivers and water courses. The country is a series of extensive prairies, slightly undulating and rising considerably as you approach the mountains. The absence of trees is not due, in my opinion, to high winds, as is supposed, in this place and the western country generally, but to the devastation which results from the savage custom of annually setting fire to the prairies. This is evident from the fact that many trunks of trees are now seen in a petrified state. Immediately east of the mountains the plains are generally covered with a meagre and hard herbage, as also with heaths, wormwood, and artemis.

"However far he may proceed, the traveller always finds himself in the middle of an immense circuit—all around is the same landscape, the same weeds, and the same flowers, and at night he seems to sleep on the same spot where he passed the previous night. The plains are intercepted by rivers and sloughs, and the necessity of crossing these, add to the inconvenience and dangers of the journey. The undulations are formed by sand hills or different kinds of rock, and vary in height from 50 to 4, or 500 feet. The ground falls gradually to the East. The uniformity of these vast solitudes is only broken by a few sandy mountains, united in confused masses, a few rocky heights or frightful ravines which cut across them. The trees commonly seen on the streams are willows, poplars, cotton trees, elm, oaks, wild plum trees, and a few fruit bushes, wormwood and artemis are the predominant productions of the great plains, but in the valleys of the rivers are also chesnuts, ash, Chinese lilacs, mesquites and willows, under the trees there grow neither bush nor thicket, and the ground is overgrown with long grass and verdant moss. Such are the general features of this wild, solitary region, which may be compared to the steppes of Asia, and in which everything makes a deep impression on man and strikes him with awe. Buffaloes, panthers, antelopes, otters, beavers, turkeys, grouse, quail, and partridges inhabit these plains. In all that portion south of 30 degrees of latitude, the air is pure and sweet, and the climate deliciously mild. The sky is as blue as an oriental sapphire, and a gentle breeze ever plays over it, bearing upon its wings the fragrance of flowers. In passing over the plain, the geological configuration of the soil changes completely. From the Rio Grande to the Rio Rouge are seen large rocks of lime and gypsum from the common plaster of Paris to the purest selenite—then granite replaces these, then quartz, felspar and mica are seen, as well as quantities of petrifactions.

"One of the singular and interesting sights on my route was the villages of the Prairie dogs. These were always found in elevated and uncovered spots. Some of them were twenty miles across. The Prairie dog resembles a squirrel in shape, size, and physiognomy. His bark, which is the only thing he has in common with the real dog, has given him his name. He burrows in the ground, excavating to the depth of from eight to ten feet, the earth it throws up being afterwards built in the form of a cone over his subterraneous abode. A large part of the day, during pleasant weather, the dogs sit on the summit of these dwellings apparently chattering together. A few sentinels are posted to give warning of approaching danger.

When an enemy is seen advancing, they bark in a peculiar way, and the entire community of dogs disappear under the earth. The Prairie dog lives apparently without water, always selecting dry situations for the towns. They close the entrance to their dwellings with dry grass at the beginning of winter, and fall to sleep till the return of spring.

"The interest created by the natural beauties, the landscapes, and the wild poesy of these immense plains, was small compared to that aroused by the numerous evidences on the route of a previous and extinct civilization. Of course, I can form very little idea as to the people to whom these antiquities ought to be attributed; but they are evidently the work of different nations, at different epochs. These tumuli consist of conical shaped mounds and pyramidal hillocks. Though it was important that I should proceed with every despatch upon my hazardous journey towards the east, I delayed two hours to make an excavation, with the assistance of Charles, into one of these rare mounds near the Rio Rouge. I took from this tumulus some bones, shells, and pieces of pottery, which indicate in those by whom they were manufactured a certain knowledge of art. The shells, curious to say, are marine, and unlike any I have ever seen in America or the West Indies; are similar to those brought you from China by Dr. Peyton. The mounds are evidently the sepulchral tombs or burial places of former generations. Built of earth, and covered with grass and trees, they much more readily resist the ravages of time, than monuments built of stone. I am much mistaken if antiquarian research does not show that ages previous to the discovery of America by Columbus, this continent was inhabited by people of an advanced civilization, as compared with the Red Skins of to-day. I shall not, however, enter upon a question so arduous in these hurried letters, but reserve much that I have to say in this connection till my return. The discovery of these things had a powerful and pleasing effect upon my mind. Something, (when I considered that I might be traversing the oldest rather than the newest world,) of the same kind of feeling with which one might be supposed to tread the ground which Abraham trod; where Nahor the father of Rebecca lived; and of Laban, to whom Jacob fled to avoid his brother Esau's resentment, and whom he served fourteen years for the love he bore Rachael.

"In the few lines I have dashed off on this subject, I have not undertaken to describe even generally, still less, step by step, those vast solitudes over which I have just come. To describe nature in such boundless regions, where nature changes its aspect at every moment, and where the traveller is struck alternately with admiration and awe at the extraordinary phenomena, would be as laborious and fatiguing as a journey across them. For the present I content myself with this rapid glance."

CHAPTER XIII.

HE ARRIVES AT THE MOUTH OF THE KENTUCKY RIVER.—DEMOCRATIC SENTIMENTS IN THE BACKWOODS SETTLEMENT.—VISIT TO AN INDIAN TOWN.—MAMMOTH BONES.—ANTIQUITIES.—ASPECT OF THE COUNTRY.—DEFEAT OF A FRENCH AND INDIAN FORCE BY THE CHICKASAWS.

NEARLY two months transpire between the date of the last of the St. Louis letters, and that which follows, written in Kentucky on the 21st of July, and the 12th and 18th of August, 1774. The conclusion of this letter is destroyed; but as it doubtless referred to the Indian tribes of the Ohio, who are better known now than then, its loss is comparatively of little importance. During this period, my grandfather was making his way through the Wilderness, in the direction of Virginia.

"A journey of twenty-eight days brought me from the south-western part of the province of Kentucky, where I was delayed by an attack of fever and ague, of which I gave you an account in my letter of the 2nd inst.* to this place. Having been directed to the house of Mr. Henderson, he received and entertained us in the most hospitable manner. He is the owner of a large and fertile plantation on the Kentucky river, and lives in the midst

* This letter is missing.

of plenty, if not of peace. During my sojourn, we have visited together the different settlements in the vicinity, which present every evidence of prosperity and happiness. The Kentuckians, however, anticipate at an early day an Indian war, and are already making extensive defensive preparations. They have erected three stockade forts to protect themselves and families. I was surprised to find, however, that these forts were not in supporting distance of each other, and not to be held against a numerous and determined enemy in possession of the open country : that such an army might completely invest them, and thus compel their capitulation. At the instance of a committee of the inhabitants, I made a reconnaissance of the country, and soon found admirable spots for the erection of forts ; and by means of three, I imagined a section lying between the Ohio and Kentucky rivers, of 1,500 acres, could be easily defended. The country covered by these forts ; would also enable the inhabitants to protect from capture their herds of horses, cattle, sheep and swine. The plans I furnished them for these works, were selected from a number, the peculiar value of which, for defence against the Indians, Colonel de Blois had pointed out to me. They are very simple, but I am persuaded will answer the purposes of defence against the savages, especially if they are constructed of stone and earth, which will render them fire-proof, as I earnestly represented to the authorities they should be. Every dwelling-house and out-building in this settlement is built of logs covered with boards. These houses are proof against Indian bullets, but the savages have learned to destroy them by means of arrows wrapped with dried grass, and steeped in the resinous exudations of the pine tree. Firing these arrows, they shoot them upon the roofs of the buildings, which are quickly in flames.

"No sooner were the spots for the forts indicated, and the committee supplied with plans and instructions for their building, &c., than they devised a scheme for their immediate erection. No one in the settlement had ever seen a regularly constructed fortification, nor was there any one among them with the slightest pretensions to military knowledge. Comprehending at once, however, the advantages of such works as those suggested, they set to work to build them with the greatest zeal, energy and public spirit. I hope they will meet with entire success, though in every undertaking they are obstructed by the prevalent western want of subordination to authority. Absolute equality prevails in all ranks in the backwoods. No deference is paid except from the weaker to the stronger, from the timid to the bold. Every public work proceeds slowly, and is constantly in danger of being abandoned from a misunderstanding among the workmen. In times of public peril, there is great reason too to apprehend from this cause anarchy and confusion.

"For mutual protection and convenience, the inhabitants of this particular settlement have voluntarily adopted a code of laws for the government of their community. This code was prepared by my worthy host, who is possessed of considerable learning, and is moreover skilled in the law. Having a copy of the Virginia statutes, he has epitomized, simplified and adapted them to the use and police of the community The people have chosen him their chief magistrate, and given him extensive powers. Thus no one elected to office, even by the people, can serve without the sanction and approval of the chief magistrate. By these modified statutes all officers are elected by the people, who vote *viva voce*. Three magistrates are chosen to serve with the chief magistrate, and all disputes which are not settled by them are submitted to a jury of eighteen, chosen from the elders by the people, to serve twelve months. If the decision of the jury is distasteful to either litigant, an appeal lies to the chief magistrate whose judgment is final in cases of this kind. From these facts, it is evident that while the republican ideas of these Kentuckians is such, that they will not acknowledge an absolute ruler, alleging that they have left the eastern and southern colonies to free themselves from the tyrannical power of His Majesty George III.; the every day necessities of their situations (*necessitas non habet leges*) have driven them to elevate from among their own number, one whose authority is somewhat despotic. With few exceptions, the inhabitants are Virginians, recruited from the most adventurous, spirited and energetic of our population. They do no discredit to the old dominion. All manly virtues are cultivated by them, and pusillanimity, cowardice and mean spirit is unknown.

" During one of the many horseback excursions taken with Mr. Henderson, we visited the confluence of the Kentucky and Ohio rivers. At that point the Ohio is nine hundred yards wide, and the Kentucky four hundred. The soil on both rivers is dark brown, almost black and very fertile, the soil of the hills is of a reddish brown colour and is covered with a lofty growth of straight trees. The forest of Kentucky consists of yellow and white poplar, walnut, red bud, hiccory, oaks of many different kinds, gum, sycamore, maple, horn-beam, dog wood, pine, chesnut, beach, holly, cedar, sassafras, wild cherry and many other descriptions peculiar to the country, and all of extraordinary size. Our chief object in visiting the confluence of the rivers was to examine some skeletons, which a party of hunters had discovered there, and which were reputed to be the skeletons of elephants. Upon examining the bones, we were both of the opinion that they belonged to some gigantic animal now extinct, and not of the elephant species. For no elephants have ever been discovered in either North or South America, nor in any part of the world of a size and magnitude which these bones indicate. Neither are the bones of the feet, in the monster skeletons here found, so flat as in the foot of the elephant, and the vertebrae of the neck much longer. To what gigantic species of quadrupeds they belong, I am at a loss to imagine. Their discovery opens an interesting field of investigation for the naturalist and philosopher.

"The Ohio which is much the larger stream, is confined to its channel by two banks, the upper and lower, on either side. When the river is low during the comparatively dry season of summer, the water is confined within the lower banks, during which period the current being smooth and gentle, canoes, barges and batteaux ascend the stream during the spring and autumn floods; when the river is swollen to the edge of the upper bank and the current is strong and rapid, boats, barges and so forth descend, sometimes travelling one hundred and fifty miles a day. At this season it is common for boats to descend from Pittsburg to New Orleans, finding the channel nowhere in a distance, not far from 2,500 miles, less than twenty-five feet in depth. Vessels of heavy draught may therefore navigate the interior of the continent, and the industrial and commercial importance of this fact cannot be overestimated. The valley of the Mississippi is destined to become the home of millions, probably hundreds of millions of human beings, and the seat of possibly the grandest empire the world has ever seen.

"These rivers, as indeed all I have crossed east of the Rocky Mountains, abound in fish. Many of these fish are very fat and of extraordinary size, such as the cat-fish, which not uncommonly weighs between one and two hundred pounds. Throughout Kentucky, game abounds and the deer are merely killed for their skins. Elk are also numerous, and buffaloes, wolves, bears, foxes, racoons, and opossums. On the rivers almost every variety of water-fowl is to be found. Sometimes in the savannahs as many as six thousand turkeys have been seen in a single flock."

"August 12th.

"I have now been with my kind Kentucky friend three

weeks, during which period my health has much improved. I leave to-morrow morning for Virginia. My excellent friend insists upon my remaining longer, for the Kentuckians are as hospitable as Arabs; but I am deaf to all importunities, remembering the trite adage, 'withdraw thy foot from thy neighbour's house, lest he be weary of thee.' My impatience to see my dear mother and yourself increases also, if this be possible, as I approach home.

"During my visit here I have made many excursions up and down the river, and find everything in tranquillity, and the Indians quiet and friendly. Nevertheless, apprehensions still exist among the whites, of a war. Mr. Henderson, Mr. MacGowan and myself have visited several Indian towns, one belonging to the Miniamis or Tweetwees, and another to the Shawnese. Nothing peculiar was discovered in their manners and customs, and all seemed friendly. The Indians who have come in contact with Europeans, however, are so crafty, suspicious, vindictive and withall so full of courage and duplicity, that the whites do not readily trust to friendly appearances. I mention where they have come in contact with the whites designedly, for it is admitted by all travellers among them, yourself, dear father, among the number, that where uncorrupted by this association, they are kind, hospitable and inspired by just and noble sentiments. They have been so often deceived; treated with such treachery and barbarity, that their souls thirst for revenge, and there is nothing which the savage will neglect to gratify this passion. He has been known to travel 500 miles on foot, through the forest, in the darkness of night, concealing himself by day, to avenge a wrong. This deep-rooted determination to revenge his injuries, has led to his great caution and his rare powers of dissimulation. And here on the frontier he has greater opportunities for displaying these qualities. I must not forget to say, however, what I have discovered from personal observation, that the Indian when a friend, is a steady and warm friend. We know this to be true among those in Virginnia, and it is confirmed by the whites of those in the West."

"August 18th.

"Having made my preparations to leave Kentucky and proceed by the river in a batteau, secured through Mr. MacGowan from a Chickasaw Indian, who agreed to accompany me and act as boatman, I bid adieu to my kind and excellent friends and went aboard the 15th of August 1774. My Chickasaw boatman soon proved a truly valuable acquisition, knowing the river well and speaking the language of the wild hoardes on either shore. The Chickasaws are a brave tribe, distinguished throughout this country for their virtue and indomitable spirit. They are tall and well formed, very strong and active, with handsome features, expressive countenances and generous souls. Our allies, no arts of the French have ever seduced them from their duty and allegiance. On one occasion to bring them to terms, the French dispatched from Canada a thousand of their best troops, supported by 2,500 Indians; but notwithstanding the disparity in numbers, they met such determined resistance from this heroic race, that they were totally defeated. Not more than 100 French found their way back to Canada."

(The end of this letter is missing.)

CHAPTER XIV.

HE ARRIVES ON THE GREAT KENEWHA RIVER.—MEETS AND JOINS THE ARMY OF GENERAL LEWIS.—TAKES PART IN THE BATTLE OF POINT PLEASANTS.—ACCOUNT OF THE BATTLE AND SKETCH OF GENERAL LEWIS AND OF THE LAMENTED COLONEL CHARLES LEWIS.—IS WOUNDED AND REMOVED TO THE GREENBRIER.

THE following letter dated at the residence of his friend, Colonel Andrew Lewis, on the Greenbrier River, October 30, 1774, is one of a number addressed to his father subsequent to his departure from the Kentucky settlement. The others are lost. This is greatly to be regretted. They were doubtless letters detailing, in full, the events connected with the operations of the army, under General Lewis, which culminated in the magnificent victory of Point Pleasants, on the 10th of October, 1774, of which a meagre account is contained in this chapter. As such, they could have possessed no ordinary interest.

"You will understand fully the causes of my disappointment and delay, in proceeding up the Kenewha from my letters of the 20th and 25th of Augnst, and the 15th and 20th of September, forwarded by Mr. Samuel Green.*

* These letters are missing.

I hasten now to give you some account of myself since the date of the last letter. Providing myself, Charles and Annetta with good rifles in exchange for our Spanish muskets, which we lost in the manner mentioned; ammunition and Indian dresses, consisting of hunting shirts, buckskin leggins and moccasins, which are the most convenient for travelling; as also blankets to sleep on and to cover us, during the time we should have to sleep in the woods, also horses with bells suspended from their necks to enable us to hear them at a distance, when they were turned loose to feed, and hobbles made of strong thongs of leather to prevent their wandering, we struck off in the direction of the head waters of the Kenewha, travelling the war path which has been immemorially used by the Indians. The savages who had recently come down this way, reporting to their confederates, the Shawnees, Mingos and Delawares, north of the Ohio, the preparations of the Virginians to send a force against them; left the road open to us. The great and lasting services rendered by my faithful Chickasaw, in ascertaining the situation of these Indians and their intentions, I shall never be able properly to recompense. I parted with him, with no small regret, but his engagements required that he should return, having agreed to accompany a gentleman to New Orleans. Two such faithful, intelligent, and courageous attendants as Charles and himself, it would be difficult to find. They belong to the class of men who are not inappropriately styled nature's noblemen. Annetta, too, has proved worthy of her husband, and during my illness has watched and tended me, as she is now doing with the care and tenderness of a mother. Though dowerless when she married Charles, except in her beauty, her virtues and her gentleness, she will prove a prize beyond value to him. 'A virtuous woman, her price is far above rubies.' It seems almost incredible that one so young and apparently fragile, who had never been from home longer than a day till she set out with us, could have had strength and spirit to make the wonderful journey of between two and three thousand miles, we have accomplished. A journey through a wilderness without adequate supplies, with no sufficient protection against the weather and a considerable part of which was on foot.

"She not only did this, but without a day's illness, or any perceptible effect upon her health. Her thin aquiline features may have gained an additional degree of sharpness, her yellow skin may have become a trifle more sallow, but if so, this was all. Her spirits were uniformly cheerful, and no murmur escaped her lips. While she bore the journey thus, I was repeatedly ill with fever and rheumatism, and Charles was twice unable to proceed for five days together. She had made up her mind, however, to accompany us at every hazard, impelled by her devoted affection for Charles, and her warm attachment to myself, as well as by a determination to desert the household of a brutal father and a cruel step-mother. She has never once, in the midst of the desert, of night and the storm, expressed a regret at her course, but having turned her back upon her degraded family and distant country, has resolved to follow after him in the spirit of Ruth: 'whither thou goest, I will go; and where thou lodgest I will lodge; thy people shall be my people, and thy God my God.' She wishes him, however, instead of returning to Jamaica, to continue in my service, and make Virginia his home. Nothing would please me more, but whatever course they pursue, I shall charge myself through life with their protection, and if necessary, their support. I owe more than this to them—in fact everything—my life indeed. In no case can I adequately repay the deep debt of gratitude and obligation I owe them. The motive which induced Charles to enter Santa Fé with naked feet, because his master was without shoes, has actuated him and Annetta in every act towards myself since we left that town— may I always be as constant to my resolution as they have been steady to their duty, *Basis virtutis constantia.*

"We kept on our course several days, travelling through an exceedingly rough country, and over the war path, which was very bad, crossing many deep streams and water courses, when we found ourselves finally beginning to ascend some of the western spurs of the great Apalachian chain of mountains. After the first night spent among them, I found my strength and spirits improving in a remarkable manner. This was obviously attributable to the salubrity and elasticity of the air. Charles and Annetta experienced the same pleasant and beneficial effects. The ascent of the mountains was exceedingly difficult and troublesome. We had often to alight from our horses. The ascent of the mountain by the war path is eight miles, and the latter part so steep as to be almost impracticable. I was repaid however for my fatigue by the prospect spread before us on attaining the summit—the perspective being wonderful and almost unbounded. No language can adequately describe the scene, which expanded the soul and filled the mind with reverential awe. Our own littleness did not, however, diminish our intellectual faculties, and the mind boldly soared over the vast extent of earth and water around, and even above the globe itself, to contemplate and admire the amazing works and mighty power of Him who had created all.

"From our elevation, we could plainly see for miles the course of the great Kenewha, up which we had travelled, and the Holston or New river where it breaks through the mountains, forming awful chasms. Also the Clinche river, or some other stream I took to be it, and the Elk. In no direction over the wide circuit where the eye wandered, was there the slightest trace of art or improvement. The entire effect was produced by nature alone, and in her sublimest forms. The scene recalled the beautiful lines of Thomson—

"'Plains immense
Lie stretched around; interminable meads,
And vast savannahs, where the wandering eye,
Unfixed, is in a verdant ocean lost.'

"After contemplating with extasy this magnificent scene, which seemed to engross the mind and enlarge the soul we commenced the descent, and towards evening, having arrived on the border of a beautiful stream, meandering through a green savannah, stopped for the night. Turning the horses loose among the succulent grass, we kindled a fire, and proceeded to roast a wild turkey, which Charles shot a few minutes before, and upon it and some dried venison, made a delicious repast, which we washed down with Kentucky whiskey, for we had brought from the Sandy a considerable stock of this excellent liquor. Wrapping ourselves in blankets, and lying down under a large tree, with our feet to the fire, we were soon asleep. In the morning we arose without the slightest dejection or oppression of spirits, but light and gay-hearted. Despatching our matutinal meal of cold turkey and venison, we proceeded down the rivulet, and coming to a deep stream near nightfall, about forty miles from our starting point, stopped on its banks for the night.

"Our supper again consisted of a roast wild turkey. These birds were now so numerous that we could easily have subsisted a hundred men upon them. We might have killed any number we chose, but having no disposition to delay our journey, or indeed to destroy them, we only shot those we required for food.

"Next morning while breakfasting, preparatory to recommencing our journey, we were startled by the report of a rifle, the bullet of which cut through Charles' hat, and had it passed an inch lower, must have cleaved his skull. The shot proceeded from a white scout on the opposite bank of the stream, who had mistaken ours for a party of Indians. This was, indeed, easily done, from our dress, and the tawny skins of Charles and his wife. Starting up and hailing the scout, I explained our true character. Meanwhile, the scout was joined by twenty others, who, apprehending we might be enemies, seeking to decoy them into an ambush, invited us to cross the stream to them, which we proceeded to do Scarcely had we arrived upon the opposite shore, when an officer approaching, to our mutual surprise and delight, we proved to be old friends. This officer was, indeed, my old and much esteemed friend, Major Charles Lewis, of Augusta County, Esquire. Hurriedly explaining to Major Lewis the nature of my adventures since leaving Virginia, and the manner in which I had arrived at this point on my return, I was greatly pleased to learn that you had received intelligence of my arrival at St. Louis. Major Lewis said he had not seen you, but had heard the fact from Dr. Mercer, of Fredericksburg. He also informed me that my adventures had become the subject of conversation among friends and relations, and the people generally, and that you were daily expecting my re-appearance at home. He then informed me, that the force in which he held His Majesty's commission as major, was composed principally of the militia of Greenbrier and border country generally, which had been raised under orders from the Earl of Dunmore,* by his brother, Colonel Andrew Lewis, who was commander-in-chief. That the Governor had marched in person at the head of another force, against the Indians in the vicinity of Pittsburg, while Colonel Lewis had been ordered to march against the enemy in this direction, far as the Ohio river, and there without crossing, to await further orders. While these explanations were going forward, I was surprised and pleased at the approach of two old friends, Major Fields, at whose house I had often been, and Captain Stewart. They were exceedingly glad to meet me, and as I was now somewhat relieved of my anxiety to push on, learning that you had received my letters, I determined, at the instance of my friends, to join their force, and serve the campaign against the savages.

"Notwithstanding the great anxiety which I know you

---

* Then the Governor of Virginia.

feel to see me, I was conscious it would give you pleasure to know I was unwilling to lose an opportunity of serving my country. That you would readily excuse additional delay in my return when you understood its cause. Although by no means applying the lines of the immortal bard of Avon to myself in their full force and significance, they recurred to memory at this moment, and were not without their influence in determining my course. 'If killed, it is but one dead that is willing to be so; I shall do my friends no wrong, for I have few to lament me; the world no injury, for in it I have nothing; only in the world I fill up a place, which may be better supplied when I have made it empty.'

"Soon afterwards I met Colonel Lewis himself, who informed me that his son, Captain John Lewis, who had been married a short time before, was too ill to accompany the expedition, notwithstanding his strong desire to do so. His company was present, but badly officered, and he said, as I was determined to join the expedition, he would give me a command in it. I gladly accepted the position of first lieutenant, and being introduced to the company, assumed the command, at the instance of the nominal captain, who had no knowledge of military matters. So much had a day brought forth, though it was now only ten of the clock, a.m.

"Colonel Lewis is, every way, an extraordinary man. His stature is gigantic, his countenance stern, and his bearing commanding, almost haughty. But 'his pride is rather on him than in him—not sinking in his heart, though ceaselessly condemned for a proud man'; and far more beneficent than he appeareth.' He is an old and distinguished soldier, having been present with Washington at the battle of Braddock's defeat in 1755,[*] and three years later in 1758, commanded the Colonial forces on the celebrated Shawanoc or Sandy Creek expedition. In fact,

[*] See Appendix A.

having been an Indian fighter from his boyhood, and a participator in every border war since.

"He is a man of great genius, and of invincible courage, perfectly acquainted with Indian warfare. He is indeed the life and soul of the troops, by whom he is esteemed, respected and beloved. To his wonderful activity and enterprise, he unites good-nature and the utmost generosity, possessing in the highest degrees that rare, I may say heavenly, turn of mind, which at peace with itself diffuses harmony and cheerfulness to all around. In the greatest excitement he is perfectly composed. No business, however urgent or difficult, no event however unexpected, no accident however sinister, ever suspended the cool tenor of his thought, deranged the presence of his mind, or ruffled the serenity of his temper. In all situations and under all circumstances, he has full dominion of himself, and no where does it give him more decided superiority than in the field. This felicity of nature is not confined to his public conduct, but attends him at the domestic hearth and the social board—everywhere the same habit of soul, which, in his public duties render him valuable to his country and formidable to his enemies, gain him the admiration and esteem of his friends and the unbounded affection of his family, and those brought in intimate association with him.

"Captain Thomas Lewis, his son, was also on the expedition, with his company. After taking command of my company, we rapidly proceeded down the Kenewha, recrossing the mountain towards the mouth of the river. Every day, however, it was evident that we were approaching nearer and nearer an Indian force. Their scouts were frequently seen at a distance, as also the smoke of their camp fires. We knew from this that they were not in large bodies, for they never allow smoke to rise from their fires, when they wish to conceal their presence, using charcoal for fuel and other devices, of which they have not a few.

"We now found that we were somewhat embarrassed

by having Annetta *en suite*, and Colonel Lewis determined to form a small camp in his rear for the sick and disabled, and to leave her there. Accordingly this was done, at a point on the Kenewha about twenty miles from its confluence with the Ohio. The wretched condition in which our camp was ordinarily kept, and the want of skill in the selection of proper spots for them, had often annoyed Colonel Lewis, and he now ordered Major Lewis and myself to select a spot for this invalid encampment. We did this after a very brief examination of the ground. The site was upon an elevated piece of ground, where there was plenty of fresh air, good drainage and excellent spring water. A heavy forest, too, protected it from the north winds. After disposing of his heavy luggage in this spot, which was formed into a kind of entrenched camp, by means of timber and earth, the sick and disabled numbering twenty, were placed in charge of it, reinforced by a non-commissioned officer and six privates. None of the enemy were yet in our rear, and it was not apprehended that the sick would be in danger; but Colonel Lewis, who is as much distinguished for prudence and forethought, as for gallantry, thought proper to provide against accident, such as might arise from small flank parties. Leaving Annetta with the party in this fort, which was called Fort Necessity, we resumed our march and proceeded ten miles down the north banks of the Great Canaway, and arrived at the junction of the two rivers, October 1, 1774. Colonel Lewis himself marked out the encampment on the banks of the Canaway, having regard to the health, comfort and convenience of the army, as well as the safety of the command. With his flanks protected by the rivers Ohio and Canaway, Colonel Lewis considered himself perfectly secure. Our sense of security was increased by intelligence received at this time, to the effect, that the Earl of Dunmore had crossed the Ohio with 9,000 men, and penetrated the Indian territory as far as the river Hockhocking. That he only waited reinforcements to penetrate into the heart of the Shawnese country and destroy their towns. When established in our camp, scouting parties were sent across the Ohio to reconnoitre. Major Charles Lewis, Captain Thomas Lewis and myself accompanied one of these parties on the second day after going into camp, scouring the country from twelve to fifteen miles in every direction, making a complete circuit of our position, without seeing any Indians, though there were many traces of the recent presence of small parties.

"On the morning of the tenth day after going into camp, we were startled by a report of musketry near the spring, from which we drew our supply of water. As our scouts had reported no enemy within fifteen miles the evening before, and no attack or alarm occurred during the night, we could not imagine the cause of this unexpected firing. From whatever cause it proceeded, least of all was it supposed to come from enemies. Instead, however, of slackening, it increased in rapidity. The alarm was beaten; trumpets and drums instantaneously broke the stillness of the morning. Their martial notes reverberated over the surrounding solitudes in enlivening strains. The ill-omened birds of night flapped their wings, and swooped through the unsteady lights of the morning in utter dismay at this untimely invasion of their prescriptive dominion. These sounds were quickly followed by the sharp discharge of musketry from the companies, as they formed in presence of Colonel Lewis, and moved into action. As this was going on, our pickets reported a large force of the enemy advancing upon us, as if they had fallen from the clouds, or sprung from the earth. The whole woods swarmed with painted warriors, armed with rifles, tomahawks, war-clubs, and battle-axes. The rapidity with which our troops prepared for battle, alone saved us from destruction, for we were taken completely by surprise, in accordance with the designs of the savages. These frontier troops, however, have been so long accustomed to the presence of an enemy, and are so skilled in savage wiles, that they are neither panic-struck by the war whoop of the Indian, nor the report of his rifle, but immediately on an alarm seize their trusty rifles, and sheltering themselves behind a tree, or rock, prepare to sell their lives as dearly as possible. Colonel Lewis, being advised of the approach of the enemy, immediately placed himself where he could personally superintend the formation of the line of battle, and moving in front of the regiments, addressed encouraging words to them in terse and forcible language, as follows:

"'Virginians! behold, yonder sky glows with a blood-red hue; it is your property rising in flames. What will you look for, if you turn back and fly? Your huts? they lie in ashes. Your wives? they are ill-treated. Your children? they are scalped and murdered. Your God? His altars are overthrown! Virginians! the day of vengeance is come. Be men, and pray to Him there above, who sends help in the hour of need.'

"These noble words were partly lost in the wild shouts of the young warriors to whom they were addressed, as their souls became excited by his lofty eloquence—just as the monotonous din of battle was occasionally broken through the day, by the shrill whoop of some young savage, whose animal spirits were aroused by the sight of blood.

"'The manner in which the Red Skins had arrived near us, and the battle begun, was as follows: The Indians who inhabit Ohio—the principal tribe being the Shawnese—having heard faithful reports from their spies and emissaries in Virginia, of the orders and movements of Earl Dunmore and Colonel Lewis, deliberately prepared to crush the force of 'Long Knives,' as they called the Virginians under Lewis, by which means they supposed the whole country, lying as far east as Staunton, in the valley of the Shenandoah, would be at their mercy for plunder during the winter. They did not so much care for Earl Dunmore's movements so far north as Pittsburg, the early approach of winter would, they supposed, put a stop to his operations, and confine him in those hyperborean regions till spring, when the warriors of the Ohio would have returned from Central Virginia, to confront him with their entire allied forces. Their spies reported Lewis' exact force, as it had arrived at the western base of the Alleghany mountains, and that he was without 'thunder guns,' as they called cannon. They also reported that he had passed beyond a point where he could receive reinforcements or supplies, and if defeated, his entire force must perish in battle, or fall as prisoners into their hands. Here was a splendid opportunity, and a grand war council was called at Shawnese town, in the Ohio territory. At this conference it was determined to invite the Delawares, Mingoes, Wyandotts, and other tribes to join them; that the dreaded Lewis (for his fame was spread among them since 1755), might be crushed at a single blow. To carry out this design the more effectually, it was determined to withdraw all Indians from Virginia, that the vigilance of the 'pale-face' chief might thereby be relaxed. Then at the right moment they would surprise, and butcher, or capture the whole force. All Indian warriors were, in accordance with this plan, withdrawn from the Canaway valley, and the allied Indians, to the number of 12,500 fighting men, assembled at Shawnese town, sixty miles west of the Ohio. These 12,500 were chiefly warriors of the Shawnese tribe, as may be supposed from having assembled at their head-quarters. A tribe, as you know, the most courageous and blood-thirsty of all within our knowledge, and the same which has so often defeated us, as in the case of Major Grant and his Scotch Highlanders at Fort Pitt, in 1758, and their defeat of the Kentuckians at Blue Lick.* This force was kept in readiness to move at an instant's warning, their horses bridled, and their rifles loaded. The utmost impatience was mani-

---

* In this engagement, the Indians killed Colonel John Todd, grandfather of Mrs. Lincoln, widow of the late President of the United States.

The Adventures of my Grandfather. 143

fested among them to move, as spies reported the gradual approach of Colonel Lewis; and while he delayed to form his camp for invalids, some difficulty was experienced to restrain their impatience, especially as the scouts reported that there was little regularity, order, or discipline among the white troops, or 'Long Knives,' who imagined no enemy was near. When, however, the Indians were informed that Colonel Lewis had halted between the two rivers, and was about to fortify that point, they moved rapidly from Shawnese town east to a point on the Ohio river, about twenty miles above our camp, from which point their horses were sent back. Here they crossed a river, more than two miles wide, with a channel twenty-five feet deep, without boats, canoes, ships, or bridges, after the following manner. With their tomahawks they constructed rafts from the trees growing on the banks of the stream, and thus transported themselves, their arms and ammunition to the Virginia shore. When upon the same side of the river with ourselves, each warrior carrying sufficient dried venison for a week's support, they concealed themselves in the woods during one day. As night approached, they commenced their march towards our camp by different routes, and conducted it in such secrecy and skill, that the whole force was near daybreak within one mile of our camp fires without its having been discovered. Here the savages rested for breakfast, and until it was light enough to know how to conduct their attack. At this time, some of our men who had gone to the spring, seeing an object they supposed to be an Indian lurking in the woods, fired upon him, and thus the alarm was given. This was the morning of the 10th of October, 1774. Our men being hurriedly formed into companies, Colonel Lewis ordered one company to reinforce the pickets near the spring, by advancing in open order, and from tree to tree. Then a second and a third company, until our entire force was engaged on a circumference of three miles and a-half. For the savages spread around in such a manner, as almost to envelope us with their murderous fire, at the same time intoning their war songs.*

"In this manner the battle waged the entire day, the forces swaying to and fro like the ebbing and flowing tide. There was no manœuvring, no charging with the bayonets, no out-flanking, and consequently very little opportunity for a display of military skill. There was a constant fire maintained however by each party, from behind the trees and rocks, and from the ravines which swarmed with them. The whites practising Indian tactics *Fas est et ab hoste doceri.* Each party took deliberate aim whenever an opportunity presented, by a man exposing himself, and the Indians threw away little ammunition. Our troops were more prodigal. When the savages extended their lines, there was a corresponding movement on our part, and thus the battle proceeded with the greatest obstinacy. The savages were under command of their favourite chief, the intrepid and enterprising 'Cornstalk.' Through the whole day we could hear him encouraging his men, with the exclamation—' be strong—be strong.' A prisoner informed us next day, that he had killed one of his Indian warriors, in the heat of battle for retreating. It is also

---

* The battle songs of the Red Skins are stamped with such vigour of style, such choice of wild ideas and expressions, that appeal to all the sentiments of bravery and honour, that one cannot refrain from admiring them. The melody of the compound words, the brilliant energy of thought, the skill and cleverness with which the improvisator handles his language, stir up, animate and excite the passions of his auditory in a much more effectual manner than could be obtained by the finest modulations of a rhythmed music. The following are two stanzas of one of these songs translated:

"Like the war-eagle, I shall traverse the lines of my enemies;
My tomahawk and my lance shall be steeped in their blood.
Behold, my friends, what floats before my cabin,
It is the hair of the vanquished I have slain.

"O you young warriors: look with fury at the battle-field,
Dash forward, strike, kill, it is the day of vengeance,
Fear not to be reckoned among the dead,
For even then your name will be covered with glory."

thought that they were inspired with new courage, on this memorable day, by another of their great and distinguished chiefs, the well-known and dreaded Outacité, or 'the man-killer,' king of the middle and lower branches of the Cherokee nation ; but whether he was present or not is doubtful. One of our men declared that he saw him during the engagement, and that he knew him well, having met Outacité when he was in London with Sir Alexander Cummings to negotiate a treaty with George II in 1730, and again served with him twenty-eight years later under Colonel Lewis in the Shawanoe expedition of 1758.

"So brave are these Shawnese, that several times during the day, when wounded, they sallied forth from their concealment, rushed to a tree which they knew sheltered a white, and fought hand to hand with him, both using knives, till one or the other, or both fell dead.

"During the whole day Major Charles Lewis and myself had been near together, and had observed a ravine which seemed to be unoccupied by the savages, and of course undefended. A slight examination of this ravine, induced us to believe that it conducted to the rear of the Indians, and if so, it was obvious that by pursuing it, and precipitating a force upon the Indians from that quarter, the day must be ours. We determined, therefore, to represent the matter to the commander-in-chief, and to ask that an adequate force might be detailed for that duty. We accordingly made our way to him.

"When his brother, Major Charles Lewis, made known our wishes and volunteered to lead this detachment through the ravine to the attack, the commander-in-chief gave his consent. No time was lost by Major Lewis, who placed himself at the head of one hundred men, one half being of my company, and proceeded at once into the ravine. He had scarcely gone twenty yards, when he was shot dead* by five Indians who were lying in ambush. Our men instantly pursued them, and so closely, that all five were

---

* Lewis County, Virginia, was named after this gallant officer.

killed. It then appeared that they were the only savage warriors guarding this pass. Had any others been there our design must have failed. Placing a corporal and two men with Major Lewis's body, we pushed on with the utmost expedition and gained, (as we had supposed we should), the Indian rear. Here a sudden and heavy fire was opened upon their left flank and rear. Our forces in front hearing these cheering sounds, and thus knowing we had arrived at our anticipated position, immediately redoubled their exertions and rushed forward to engage the Indians hand to hand. Our wily foes, taken by surprise, gave way in somewhat of a panic, not however, without retarding our advance by many a gallant struggle, and by a steady and galling fire from tree to tree. In the midst of this terrific struggle—in which the curses and blows of the combatants were heard amid the screeches and groans of the wounded and dying, a scene more resembling the bloody contests of the gladiatorial arena, or the infuriated and sanguinary encounters of a mob, than a battle field of modern times—night came on, and both forces relaxed their exertions, as if by mutual consent, and were drawn off, the Virginians, who were the pursuers, slowly and reluctantly, the Indians in hot haste. Thus terminated, after the forces had been engaged, without relief or rest of anykind, from sunrise till dark, one of the most stubbornly contested battle-fields known to the annals of our border warfare.*

"Next morning it was ascertained that the enemy had retired across the river Ohio on their rafts, which a few warriors previously brought down the river and guarded for them, about eight miles above the battle-field.

"We had killed during this battle, 46 officers and men,

---

* In grateful recognition of Colonel, afterwards General Andrew Lewis' services on this occasion, and in many previous and subsequent battles, during the Indian wars, and that of the American Revolution, the General Assembly of Virginia decreed that his statue should be erected in the grounds of the Capitol in Richmond, where it now (1867) stands.

and 88 wounded—myself among the latter. Major Charles Lewis, though less in rank than others that were killed, is universally regarded as the principal officer slain on our side. He was a man of the highest worth and capacity, a gallant and enterprising officer, whose loss is deservedly and sadly lamented. He was greatly esteemed and the most popular man in the army, having much more suavity than his distinguished brother, Colonel Lewis.

"No one who had the opportunity of an acquaintance, no matter how limited, or how extensive in period, with the lamented Lewis could fail to feel the force of Swift's remark, "Good manners is the art of making those people easy with whom we converse; whoever makes the fewest people uneasy is the best bred man in the company." Gifted with the merits which entitled him to the esteem of the good and wise, no one possessed in a higher degree the power of making, without the slightest effort, all those 'feel easy' who came into his presence, whether upon professional business or for social intercourse. In personal appearance, he was rather beyond the middle height, with an exceedingly well-proportioned figure and strongly built frame; with features expressive of much animation, frequently inclined to a reflective or studious aspect, until lit up with a smile of peculiar brightness from an eye strongly beaming with intellect and intelligence. I concur entirely in the opinion of those who knew him best, that had his life been spared he would have rendered important, probably illustrious, service to his country. Besides Major Lewis, there was killed Lieutenant-Colonel Fleming and Lieutenant-Colonel Morrow, Captains McClanahan, Charles Cameron, Wilson and Blueford.

"After gaining the rear of the Indians, and while closely pressing them, a bullet striking a tree near me, glanced and entered my side near the hip, and passing around lodged near the spine. For some time I was paralyzed in my lower extremities, but since the ball was extracted am slowly regaining the use of my limbs. I now walk with the aid of a cane, though it will be some time, if ever, before I am an active man again.

"A few days after the battle, a messenger, named Girthy, arrived with intelligence from the Earl of Dunmore, announcing that he had overrun the Ohio territory, during the absence of the force operating against Colonel Lewis, burnt the towns and destroyed their crops. The Indians were reduced to such a pitiable condition, that on receiving the news of Lewis' victory, they sued for peace in abject terms.

"Though suffering excruciating pain from my wound, I preferred the possibility of death, from being transported, to remaining in camp. Colonel Lewis therefore detailed a force to convey me in a kind of ambulance to the mountains. I was fetched across in a litter and thence in a waggon to this place, which is called the Greenbrier settlement. I do not think the journey did me any injury, on the contrary, my general health is improved. Every one showed the utmost attention to my comfort and convenience, especially my servants, Charles and Annetta, who are now watching by me. I have every attention that could be desired here, and will soon be able to proceed homewards."

CHAPTER XV.

HE LEAVES THE WARM SPRINGS.—MOUNTAIN SCENERY.—BEAUTIFUL CASCADE.—LEGEND.—ARRIVES AT STAUNTON AND PROCEEDS TO NORFOLK.—THE POLITICAL AGITATIONS PRECEDING THE AMERICAN REVOLUTION.

In the two letters brought together in this chapter, the first dated at the Warm Springs in Augusta County,* November 1st, and the second at Norfolk, November 26th, 1774, my grandfather gives an interesting account of the political agitations immediately preceding the American Revolution. With the exception of a brief note announcing his arrival in Alexandria, these letters close the series as to him.

"After a short sojourn in the Greenbrier settlement (rendered necessary by the fatigues of the journey in my enfeebled condition), from the mouth of the Canaway, I proceed homeward, crossing the Alleghany mountains, and descending into the valley of Jackson's river. Crossing this stream, we soon came upon the celebrated cascade in the Falling Spring valley.* To visit this wonderful spot gave us little trouble, as it lies near the highway, which is, however, nothing more than the Indian war path, which has been immemorially used. This path

---
* Now Bath County.
* This is the cascade which has been known for the last half century and more as Peyton Falls.

conducted us to the top of the mountains hereabouts, which are spurs of the Alleghanies, and after a variety of turnings through peaks and chasms of stupendous height and awful aspect, we began to descend, and entered the most delightful valley I ever beheld, deep, long, and from a half to two miles in breadth, surrounded with enormous piles of mountains of savage wildness. The banks of the streams were covered with all sorts of wild flowers, the perfume of which, especially the wild thyme, was wafted through the air by gentle breezes, making our progress all the more agreeable. On the mountain sides there were large patches of arbutis, and the lauristina and other shrubs, and different kinds of flowers cherished in our gardens at Stoney Hill.

"Turning from the road, we soon arrived in view of the cascade, which is formed by a bold stream called the Falling Spring, which rushes over a ledge of limestone and tufa 250 feet high. It is the most romantic and beautiful sight I ever witnessed. Gazing upon it, I felt my heart overwhelmed with sensations of transport, which all the works of art could never inspire. Nature irresistably seized upon and took my senses captive. I acknowledged the supremacy of nature. All human associations were forgotten, as I looked upon this wonderous scene and the surrounding mountains in their marvellous magnitude and grandeur, as the work of the Almighty architect of the Universe, who can restrain the waters within their limits, uphold the rocks upon their bases, and prescribe the bounds of worlds of stars on their airy flight in the heavens. So extensive are the mountains here, so broken in varied and beautiful forms, they look down from their dizzy height upon such a bright and luxuriant valley, and assume such varied and charming tints, as they change their colour and appearance under the shadow of each passing cloud, that I felt I had never looked upon the like before. I viewed them with silent admiration, and with that submission with which weak man depicts to himself the Throne of the Almighty Creator.

"About a half-mile below the Fall, there is a powder-mill, protected by two stockade forts, from which the border country is supplied with ammunition. It is constantly in motion, and the powder is said to be of superior quality. The nitre employed is procured from the numerous caverns close at hand.

"Of this spot the following story is related by the mountaineers:

LEGEND OF THE POWDER-MILL NEAR PEYTON FALLS.*

"A solitary man once lived near this beautiful cascade, in a retired thatched cabin. He subsisted upon wild fruits and berries, upon fish taken from the stream, and the game which abounded in valley and forest. His venerable appearance and mysterious character long protected him from the red men, who left him in peace, contemptuously calling him *squaw*, while they sought in battle those with arms in their hands.

"One night this lonely dweller, near the fountain of sweet waters, had the good fortune, so runs the account, to entertain an angelic visitor. They passed half the night in delightful conversation. The visitor expatiated with heavenly wisdom upon the value of virtue and confidence in God. Before leaving the next morning, however, to the consternation and surprise of the host, he seized a flaming brand, and set fire to the thatch hut which was completely devoured by the flames. The poor mountaineer was inconsolable at his loss, and still more grieved at the wanton cruelty and base ingratitude of one whom he had entertained, and from whose lips he had heard such lessons of wisdom and piety. He no longer believed him a good spirit, neither did he place trust in his beautiful stories. His visitor gone and the ashes cool, he exclaimed: 'Courage, away with despair. I will build me a house

---

* This legend is evidently of German paternity, was no doubt carried to the Apalachian wilds by some Teutonic exile from Fatherland.

with my own hands, though it be rough and rude, yet if I have a roof I shall be content.' And behold! as he began the work, he discovered in the old foundation wall an immense treasure, so that he could bring labourers from afar, and build a substantial residence to protect himself from the storms, and still have riches left to erect a mill to supply the few feeble whites with powder to fight against the powerful and savage hordes of blood-thirsty Indians who swarmed around. He then recognized the benefaction of his visitor, and believed in the wisdom and goodness of God all the days of his life."

"Both Captain Lewis and myself are much improved by the mineral waters. I think my health also would be much benefitted by rest and the quiet of home. This is my only hope of ever being an active man again.

"Besides, I am satisfied from conversations I have recently had with many intelligent gentlemen, that the country is on the verge of civil war, and am anxious to be where I can better watch the march of events. The ill-advised act of the Ministry last year, in placing a vessel in the Narraganset, to enforce the collection of duties, and the destruction of tea the past December on board three English sloops at Boston; the Boston Port bill of this year, and Dr. Franklin's return to Europe, as well as many other symptoms, such as meetings of the people to elect committees of public safety, to call conventions, congresses, and the like, indicate that we are approaching a period of open hostilities. Even in this distant part of the country, anonymous hand-bills have been distributed and pasted against the walls in public places, calling upon the people to assemble and consider of the public danger.

"It is greatly to be regretted that Ministers have not been taught wisdom by experience. When in 1765 they sought most unjustly to throw a portion of the burden of English taxation upon our shoulders by the stamp act, and we refused to submit to it, they ought to have had sufficient wisdom, discernment and magnanimity to abandon a dangerous policy. The people said plainly enough at that time, that they were willing to pay the expenses of their own government, but would not endure to be taxed by a foreign body like the British Parliament, situated 3,000 miles across the ocean from us, in whose deliberations we had no voice, and when the very taxes we paid (if we submitted to such tyranny), might be used for hostile purposes against our freedom and security. I repeat, when the people of the Colonies showed so fully their feelings and purposes in 1765, Ministers now have no excuse for their obstinacy in adhering to and repeating such irritating demands. It only gives agitators an opportunity to inflame the public mind and widen the breach. If the Ministry persist, the cry will resound throughout the colonies that 'resistance to tyrants is obedience to God.' It is most unfortunate that the Ministry should have pertinaciously adhered to their unpopular policy, with the lights of experience before them, and laid a tax in 1767 upon tea, paints, glass, &c., and still more singular, that they persist now with all the pregnant signs of the times before them in so suicidal a course. Matters have gone so far that I shall be surprised if war does not result."

"Norfolk, November 25th, 1774.

" Shortly after the date of my last letter, I was much pleased to have a call from our old friend Dr. Hugh Mercer of Fredericksburg,* a physician of great merit and eminence, who has been some weeks in the mountains. He has given me much advice and assistance, and took charge of me from the Warm Springs to this point. To-morrow he continues his journey, and will deliver this letter in person. I shall not remain here to recover from my fatigues longer than three days. Dr. Mercer will give you more satis-

* Dr. Mercer abandoned the healing art during the American Revolutionary war and rose to the rank of Brigadier-General in the Continental Army. He was killed at the battle of Prineton, New Jersey, January 3rd, 1777.

factorily than I can in a brief letter the details of my situation since the battle at the Point, and what prospect, if any there be, of my entire restoration.

"From the Springs to Staunton the road is exceedingly rough and rocky, and notwithstanding the advanced period of the year, the heat oppressive. Staunton is a considerable town, which was founded about the year 1730 by the father of Colonel Andrew Lewis, John Lewis Esq., who was the first European who penetrated into this country. It is situated on 'Lewis Creek,' a small tributary of the Shenandore. The valley is remarkably fertile between the South Mountain or Blueridge and North Mountain, and is sometimes called the Shenandore Valley. This valley is almost entirely settled by people from Ireland. Mr. Lewis, the founder, is not now living, having died here in 1762, at an advanced age.*

"The people of Staunton carry on a large inland trade, the principal parts of which is in the hands of two merchants, natives of Ireland, George Mathews, and Samson Mathews. These gentlemen showed me many civilities.

"The rich variety of land and water, hills and dales, wood and fields in this valley is beautiful beyond description. After crossing the Blueridge or South Mountain, the country to the east is extremely hilly and broken, and

---

* John Lewis was buried on his estate now called Bellefontaine, and the following is the inscription upon his tomb, which the writer has seen within seven years.

Here lie the remains of
JOHN LEWIS,
Who slew the Irish Lord, settled Augusta county,
Located the town of Staunton
And furnished five sons to fight the battle of the
AMERICAN REVOLUTION.
He was son of Andrew Lewis, Esq., and Mary Calhoun,
And was born in Donegal county, Ireland, 1678
And died in Virginia, February 1st, 1762.
He was a brave man, a true patriot, and
A firm friend of liberty throughout
THE WORLD.
Mortalitate relicta, vivit immortalitate inductus.

the land generally lighter and less rich than in the valley. Commonly of a bright red colour, it recalled the soil in many parts of Jamaica, which it much resembles. The three days I had allotted for my sojourn in Staunton having passed, I proceeded (without stopping to see a remarkable cavern near the town, and which is said to penetrate a great way into the earth); to the mountain and crossed over to Charlottsville, feeling less fatigued than I expected. Though having much need of rest and tranquillity, I only remained in that village one night and two days. The inn there, kept by a person bearing the name of Sneed, is excellent. Political sentiment runs very very high there, and the day after my arrival the populace tarred and feathered one of the inhabitants who had expressed what are now called treasonable opinions. The general impression prevailing that he was a British spy. Already the public mind is so bent upon resistance to the Ministry, that to defend them is termed treason. The town is situated about two miles from a very pretty river, though the water of it, instead of being bright and crystal, like that north of the Blue Ridge, is yellow and turbid, taking its colour from the soil. The weather now became wet, stormy and disagreeable, yet I determined to continue my journey. Finding a heavy snow lying on the ground twenty miles east of Charlottsville, I turned from my course and proceeded towards Richmond. The only halt I made was one day at Westham, a small town on the James, about seven miles above Richmond, where the falls of the James commence. The tobacco of the West country is floated down to Westham in hogsheads of 1,000 pounds weight each. Every hogshead upon two canoes lashed together; it is then conveyed on land to Richmond, as for seven miles the fall completely precludes all communication by water. Richmond is not however the principal centre of the tobacco trade of America, but Petersburg or Bollings Point, as it is generally called. You remember in the account I gave you two years ago, of a visit I made to that very enterprising man Mr. Bannister, who lives in so palatial a residence, and such royal style at Petersburg, I mentioned the Bollings, who, as you know, are descended from King Powhatten, through his daughter the Princess Pocahontas.

"The Indian king gave all the land round Petersburg to his daughter, as a marriage portion. The offspring of this marriage are two of the most respectable Virginia houses, the Bollings' and Randolphs.

"Without stopping in Richmond to see any friends but Colonel de Blois, I took a boat in which he sailed with me for Norfolk. Language cannot describe the emotions of pleasure it gave me to sail once more after so long an absence, upon the smooth bosom of our noble river James. In my trip down, we delayed a short time at Varina, the seat of Mr. Ryland Randolph, as also at Chatsworth to see Mr. William Randolph, and at Mr. Mayho's where Colonel de Blois wished to see a friend. Everybody was prodigiously astonished to see me, though they had heard of my safe return to St. Louis.

"Leaving Mr. Mayho's we pursued our way down the river. How many happy memories were revived as we passed successfully those splendid seats of hospitality and refinement which fringe the banks of the James and at many of which I had passed some of the happiest days of my boyhood. Shirley Hundred, Brandon, Flower de Hundred, Maycox, Swineyards, Westover, Barclay, Bermuda Hundred, Osborns, Warwick Mills, &c. &c.*

"What memories too were awakened in passing the ivy draped ruins of James Town. The ruins of this sacred spot are hallowed in my mind. It represents another world of the past. From the powerful effect of the association of ideas as I looked upon the vacant places, the departed

---

* These valuable mills and iron works were entirely destroyed during the American revolutionary war, in the year 1781 by the traitor Benedict Arnold, who deserted from the American Army, and was commissioned a General in the British service.

generations who flourished here in the early days of the colony, flocked back upon me. I saw them hurrying to and fro in all the activity of every day life, intent as men ever are upon the little objects of the hour. A sort of spiritual phantasmagoria swept on before my inward vision, displaying to my wondering eyes the vicissitudes of Time. Then came the solemn thought that those men and the thousands that followed them have been swallowed up in death. How these thoughts speak to us, if we would but listen in a language of earnest warning, whispering the sage advice, 'whatsoever thy hand findeth to do, do it with all thy might, for there is no knowledge or device in the grave whither we are all hastening.' Man lives his brief span of life—dies and is forgotten. Oh! vanity of vanities! all is vanity!

"As I looked upon the site of James Town, and took in review the history of its settlement, the prominent figure and leading character, which rose before my mind, was the redoubtable Captain Smith, that wonderful man, to whose courage and endurance we owe the settlement of our colony, and whose honoured ashes repose in the heart of our old home.*

---

* From Stowe's 'Survey of London,' printed in 1633, two years after the death of Captain Smith, it appears that a tablet was erected to his memory in St. Sepulchre Church, Skinner Street, London, where Captain Smith was buried, inscribed with his motto, *Vincere est vivere*, and the following verses:

"Here lies one conquer'd who conquer'd kings,
Subdu'd large territories and done things
Which to the world impossible would seeme,
But that the truth is held in more esteeme.
Shall I report his former service done
In honour of God and Christendome,
How that he did divide from Pagans three
Their heads and lives types of his chivalry,
For which great service in that climate done,
Brave Sigismundus (King of Hungarion),
Did give him a coat of arms to weare
Those conquer'd heads got by his sword and speare.
Or all I tell of his adventures since
Done in Virginia that large continence,
How that he subdu'd kings unto his yoke,

"On the Lower James, nearly opposite the Williamsburg landing, the seat of my venerable Alma Mater, I fell in with a small sailing boat, in which was the Hon. Peyton Randolph who left Williamsburg the same day for Norfolk. We continued together till our arrival here, he having come aboard my barge. He is greatly incensed against the Ministry, and in the event of a breach, will no doubt take the prominent part to be expected from one of his acknowledged spirit and ability.

"Public spirit and ardent love of liberty pervades all classes of the people—seems to be a chief characteristic of our society. So far as my observation extends, all shades of character and opinion are rapidly assimilating and concentrating against submission to the acts of the Ministry. The most prominent characteristic of this feeling is an unreserved reliance upon the cheerful and hearty co-operation of the whole body of the citizens in the public welfare, derived from a conviction of the intimate union of all ranks and interests in the common weal. The different interests which divide other countries, and which are united by no common and original tie do not exist here. With us, every interest is bound together by a single cord; and all feel if this were broken they should be involved in a common ruin. This invisible moral power, which extends to every class, will always be conspicuous in free states, but nowhere, I am persuaded, does it exercise such sovereign power, as in America. And it is this

> And made those heathen flie as wind doth smoke,
> And made their land, being so large a station
> A habitation for our christian nation,
> Where God is glorified, their wants suppli'd
> Which else for necessaries might have di'd,
> But what avails his conquests now he lies
> Inter'd in earth a prey for worms and flyes,
> O may his soul in sweet elisium sleepe
> Until the Keeper that all souls dothe keepe,
> Return to judgment and that after thence
> With angels he may find his recompense."

The tablet was destroyed by the Great Fire in 1666, together with most of the antiquities of the church.

power, which is stronger than cannon, than any mere mechanical power, which the Ministry have arrayed against them, and must combat. There seems to be a well-founded popular belief that the political character of a nation is the genuine offspring of its constitution, that a powerful government operates to restrain the genius and degenerate the spirit of the people. So true is this, say many well-informed gentlemen, that republican families who have been transferred to a despotic soil, have lost their ardour and energy, and in a few generations have been debased by the general corruption, into the condition of slaves. Whatever want of spirit or degeneracy to be seen in a nation, they refer to a vicious constitution or a vicious administration, of what may be in itself a good constitution. In regard to our complications, the people usually declare attachment to the British constitution and loyalty to the throne, but are resolved to resist the Ministry whatever it may cost, wherever it may lead.

"It would be well for England before involving herself and the colonies in hostilities, (counting upon colonial support and our financial embarrassments); to remember the maxims laid down by Machiavel, who among other matters warns ministers not to form sanguine expectations of the success of an invasion, from the intestine divisions of the invaded country, and never to ground their hopes of victory on the disordered state of their adversaries finances.

"I shall be detained here several days longer, awaiting the brigantine 'Il Trovatore,' Captain Langlois, which is discharging cargo, and taking in freight for Alexandria. She arrived a few days ago from Leghorn, bringing news of a great Russian victory, and the total destruction of the Turkish army, after which a peace was established between the Grand Turk and the Czar."

CHAPTER XVI.

The following letter, addressed by John Peyton, Esq., from Charlottsville, Albemarle, under date of November 8th, 1774, to his son, John Rowzée Peyton, and which belongs to the collection, will be read with no small interest in this connection.

"My dear son,
"Such was my impatience to see you, when I heard from Mr. Proctor that you were in the Greenbrier settlement, that I wrote you from Stoney Hill to meet me* in Charlottsville about the 10th of this month. I accordingly set out, notwithstanding my age and infirmities, being now in my sixty-fourth year, with your mother, who is far from being well, hoping we should meet you in this village. We crossed the country in our travelling chariot, driven by Page. The roads being deep and miry, it was difficult to get on, though I had harnessed in front of our ordinary carriage horses, your pair of blood bays. A baggage waggon followed, to fetch home your curious attachés, half friends, half servants, as you call them, and your luggage, if you possess anything beyond your wearing apparel in use. Our disappointment was sore indeed, when on arriving here we were told by Mr. Sneed that you had been gone two days. Your mother and myself

* This letter is missing.

The Adventures of my Grandfather.

fully expected to see you, and never in our lives did we experience such transports as in the prospect of pressing you to our bosoms. Mr. S. also informed us that he had heard from Mr. Carter that the snow and bad roads had caused you, after leaving this place, to take the Green Spring route to Richmond, thence to proceed home by the river. Notwithstanding the inroads made upon my feelings by the hardships and afflictions of my journey here, and my disappointment, if it pleases God to spare your life, and strengthen your constitution, and bring us together again at home, I shall still be the happiest of men.

"Thinking it probable you may stop a day or two in Richmond, I send this by my servant George, who sets off immediately, accompanied by Wyanoke, an Indian scout, entrusted by the Earl of Dunmore with despatches for the Council at Williamsburg, and who travels so rapidly that I am in hopes they will overtake you in Richmond. I trust, appreciating our very great anxiety to see you, that you will lose no time in proceeding home, where I return immediately.

"Your drafts in favour of my worthy friend Mr. Brent, of the Santa Fé Jew, Levi, and your brutal jailor, Ximines, have been presented for payment, and duly honored. Nothing but my great confidence in, and affection for you, induced me to cash such extravagant drafts, as I thought those in favour of Levi and Ximines; for they came before your letters, or a word of explanation as to your situation. Now that I know the circumstances under which they were extorted from you, I can only say, had they been ten times as large they would have been met.

"Early in the spring, we made the acquaintance of the Howes, whom I have long known by reputation. Since then, they have been upon a visit to Stoney Hill, and your mother has spent some days with them on the Occoquan. They are one of our old country families—

esteemed wherever known; just the kind of sincere, straightforward persons that one wishes to make friends of. Annie, for whom you have formed so warm a friendship, is not only a girl of great beauty and refinement, but of varied accomplishments, not the least of which, to my mind, are those of being a thorough housewife. She is of a very kind and considerate nature, and added much to my comfort and enjoyment when at Stoney Hill by her musical talents, and in reading the papers to me. I should like to see you happily married, my son, and settled near me. I need a prop in my old age. You have sown a plentiful crop of wild oats, and gathered a bounteous harvest of chaff—in a word, have seen more than enough of the world, its ups and down. Are you not satisfied with roving? I think it high time you should commence the serious business of life, and if you agree with me, and should be inclined to follow your father's advice, and commence a new career by marrying, I avail myself of this writing to say you will not be opposed by him, certainly not, if your choice for a wife should be Annie Howe.

"But I must close. Your mother warns me not to fill your head even before you get home with such projects. She writes herewith, and will be more full and particular about home matters.* I now find it very irksome, indeed painful, to use the pen any length of time. My hand trembles, and my sight is fast failing; you'll therefore excuse my brevity. With our sincerest love, and continued fervent prayers for your safe and speedy return, welfare and happiness,

"I am, my dear son,
"Your affectionate father,
"John Peyton.

"For Mr. J. Rowzée Peyton,
 "now in Richmond,
"Care of Mr. James Randolph,
 "119, Main Street."

* This letter is missing.

CHAPTER XVII.

HIS RETURN TO STONEY HILL.—POLITICAL AGITATION PRECEDING THE AMERICAN REVOLUTION.

The following letter, dated at Alexandria, December the 20th, 1774, is the last contained in this series, from the pen of my grandfather. It is little more than the simple announcement of his arrival in that place, after an absence of eighteen months. In a few concluding remarks, are contained the brief history of his subsequent uneventful career, which was terminated by his untimely death, at the early age of forty-five, 1798. Many of the foregoing letters might doubtless have been omitted, as containing nothing of special interest in themselves, as others might have been given alone for their intrinsic value. Nor was it necessary to have woven them together with a sketch which gives the entire history of the life of their author, but it is believed that they cannot but be more acceptable in their present form. Dr. Johnson remarks that he who endeavours to recommend an author, by selecting quotations, is like the pedant in Hierocles, who when he wished to sell his house, exhibited a brick as a specimen. We have thought it more judicious, recalling the Doctor's sage remark, to give this collection, so far as it exists, *in extenso*, as a knowledge of the context cannot fail as we imagine, to increase the pleasure which attaches to them.

"I hasten to advise you of my safe arrival in Alexandria. Not finding a vessel for Fredericksburg or Falmouth,* I was forced to continue to this point. This note is despatched by courier, to ask you to send your travelling chariot to Alexandria, as I can procure no suitable vehicle here in which to make the journey. I shall await with impatience the messenger's return.

"Shortly after the date of my last letter, I sailed from Norfolk in the 'Il Trovatore,' bound for this place. The wind and weather became unfavourable after we left the Bay, and were ascending the river—so much so, indeed, that we anchored off the Chotank settlement,* where we were detained twenty-four hours. After which, the storm abating, we continued up the majestic river, through a succession of the most beautiful scenery imaginable. Never before did I know how to appreciate our noble Potomac. On the Virginia side we had Colonel Phil. Lee's of Nominy, Mr. McCarty's, Mrs. Blair's, Mr. Thacker Washington's, Colonel Frank Thornton's on Marchodock, Mr. Alexander's of Boydspole, Mr. Fitzhugh's, Mr. Mercer's, Mr. Brent's, Colonel Mason's, Colonel Harry Peyton's, Mr. Lawson's, near the Occoquan, Colonel Fairfax's, Colonel Martin's, Colonel Washington's, and Mr. Alexander's; and on the Maryland side, Mr. Wolstenholmes', Mr. Clark's, Mr. Lewis', Mr. Sly's, a Catholic priest's, Mr. Compton's, Mr. Lee's, Mr. Phil. Fendalo's, Colonel Dent's, Father Hunter's, Mr. Harrison's, Colonel

---

* Falmouth is at the Falls of the Rappahannock river.
† Westmorland county, Virginia, the birth-place of the illustrious Washington.

Smallwood's, Mr. Digg's, Mr. Rosier's, Mr. Addison's, and others, whose names I cannot even mention. To describe these fine country places would require a volume, and to you I would only be describing spots which you know better than myself.

"My health has improved so rapidly, that I now walk with the assistance of my cane. I hope, and I am encouraged in this hope, by all the medical men I have consulted, that from year to year I shall feel less inconvenience from the partial paralysis under which I now labour. Still young, with a constitution originally vigorous, and my general health unexceptionable, I trust I will not always be so helpless as at present.

"The excitement which I have remarked in every part of the Colony since my return, over our relations with the mother-country, is as great in this town, if not greater, than elsewhere. Repeated meetings of the people have occurred here, subscriptions been raised, and companies drilled and equipped against the contingency of war. Among the most active persons at these meetings have been Colonel George Washington, so much distinguished in 1755 at the defeat of Braddock,* and Mr. George Mason Both have subscribed to the funds being raised more largely than any others. Colonel Washington has also signified his acceptance of the command of the first company, and suggested that the uniform should be that of his old regiment in the last war, viz, blue and buff. Of course, this company has not been avowedly raised to resist the authority of England, but for purposes of general defence. It is perfectly understood, however, with what view it and other companies are formed, and instructed in military tactics. In Alexandria there are many gentlemen of loyal sentiments, but how can they defend Ministers, a majority of whom seem to have eaten of the insane root. I am much concerned at these coming troubles, which a little

* See Appendix A.

diplomacy on the other side of the Atlantic, could so easily have averted.

> "'My soul aches,
> To know, when two authorities are up,
> Neither supreme, how soon confusion
> May enter 'twixt the gap of both, and take
> The one by the other.'"

CHAPTER XVIII.

HIS MARRIAGE,—THE FESTIVITIES.—CAPTAIN PELHAM REDIVIVUS.—MR. JIMMY JONES IN CHARACTER.—DEATH OF THE VENERABLE JOHN PEYTON.—HIS CHARACTER.—CONCLUDING REMARKS.

From the period when "my Grandfather" returned to Stoney Hill, his health improved. Had he not been so seriously wounded, his physical condition would have been higher, and his constitution more vigorous, than at any former period. His general health was, indeed, perfect. It was now obvious, however, that he would suffer a permanent spinal weakness and nervous irritability. This, however, did not prevent his taking daily exercise on horseback, nor did it depress his spirits, or prevent his engaging with zest in the social amusements of the community. He was unfitted, however, for active life, and, of course, did not resume his military studies under Colonel de Blois. From this period he occupied himself with legal studies, having in the spring of 1775 been appointed a magistrate for the county, and with books upon agriculture, to which he now turned his attention. Immediately after his return to Stoney Hill, he visited Belleville, and renewed his friendship with the Howes.

More fortunate than could have been expected, he returned to the enjoyment of her constant affection, who had clung to him through evil and good report. During all the period of his silence and absence, Annie Howe had refused to believe in his death or inconstancy. "Hope told a flattering tale," and trusting her lover (though he had never avowed his love), she would have been more or less than mortal, and wise beyond her years, had she not listened to it. They were soon affianced, with the consent and approval of both families.

Three years after the date of his letter of December, 1774, their nuptials were consummated, with all the rejoicings surrounding such affairs in colonial days as now. The ceremony was performed in Belleville Hall, and not in church, as is commonly the case in England. In those days there were few churches in Virginia, and those scores, sometimes hundreds of miles apart, and marriages were necessarily performed under the parental roof.

A month before the auspicious event, invitations were issued from Belleville to the friends and relatives of both families, and long before the wedding day Mr. Howe knew that the size of the company would exceed the capacity of Belleville, and those of the mansions of his immediate friends and neighbours. The hospitality of all the gentry within a radius of twenty miles, was, therefore, as was usual, relied on for the entertainment of the guests. In accordance with the custom of those days, the guests were informed where they would be entertained, and were quietly established against the wedding day. Mr. Howe, anxious to trespass as little as possible upon his friends, had ten or twelve timber houses built in his grounds, but these were hardly made sufficiently comfortable for the accommodation of ladies, and were principally occupied by young gentlemen. Upon the afternoon preceding the wedding night, for in those halcyon days of colonial existence weddings took place in the evening, and not in the morning as at present, the company was seen converging by every road upon Belleville. The ladies in carriages and chaises, *en grande toilette*, for the ball, and followed closely by gentlemen outriders and negro-servants in livery. The young gentlemen who came *en garçon*, approached on horseback from valley and hill, and in the dashing costume of the day, with their swords and pistols, for every one then went armed, looked not unlike the scouts of a military force. A few minutes after the company had assembled in Belleville Park, to the number of several hundred, a cavalcade was seen approaching, consisting of four coaches and thirty outriders. The front equipage was a stately old family carriage, in mourning, containing Mrs. Peyton and her daughters from Stoney Hill (her venerable husband, John Peyton Esq., had now been dead more than a year) the two next carriages fetched the immediate friends of the family. A half mile in the rear of these, a coach and four bore the groom and his best man. As the carriages drove into the grounds, they were received with cheers by the company, and with deafening shouts by the negroes, old and young, who assembled in greater force than the whites. At Belleville, as was usual on these occasions, certain apartments were set aside for the ladies, and others for the gentlemen, where they could indulge in heightening their charms by any preliminary pimping* they thought necessary. At the same time, refreshments of every kind and description were served in the grand banquetting hall.

The company having now arrived, the reader must be indulged with a slight glance at its personelle. Though large, it was almost entirely composed of relatives, friends and neighbours, giving it, notwithstanding its size, the character of a large family party, and all was mirth, fun and cordiality. Aunts, grand-aunts, uncles, cousins, step-fathers and every degree of relationship and connection was represented. Many too were the deviations from fashion and taste in the costume of some of the guests, but the girls were very pretty, and with a sort of feminine instinct, seemed to have discovered in most cases how to dress to display their charms to the best advantage. Amongst these lovely girls, Annie Howe shone far, far above them all, in the majesty of her ripened beauty. The general voice awarded her the palm for grace, beauty and attraction. Most mammas, it must be confessed, however, in giving her the preference, made a secret reservation in favour of their own daughters. The bride certainly looked fair, modest and pretty, and was unexceptionally dressed, but as she closely resembled a thousand other brides, we will make no further description of her, and we must say for the good breeding of the company she attracted no particular attention, after the general judgment pronounced her queen of beauty.

Graceful minuets, Scotch reels or as they are sometimes called "Old Virginia break downs," were the order

---

* "Primping" is an American slang word of long standing, signifying to "beautify" or "embellish" the person. See Bartletts Dictionary of American slang words.

of the night. None of the modern innovations in the way of dances were admitted, such as "flat foot waltzes" and polkas, in which hilarious young gentlemen sometimes "squeeze" their partners. The general cheerfulness was partaken of by the old gentlemen, some of whom yielded to the earnest solicitations of the youthful part of the company, and joined in a dance or two. For the most part, however, the gentlemen of the old school were holding converse in a side room over their toddy and tobacco pipes upon the favourite topic, among the old style in Virginia, family traditions, legends, genealogy and so forth.

It should have been stated, however, before all this, that the marriage procession having been formed in the boudoir of Mrs. Howe, proceeded through the grand corridor to the chapel, (for in these days in every old Virginian mansion, a room was fitted up for private devotion, called the chapel), where the ceremony was performed by the rector of the Parish, according to Annie Howe's particular request ; and not by the Rector from Stoney Hill, as would have been the usual custom. The ceremony over, which includes the subsequent congratulations, &c., the entire company proceeded to the ball room, adjoining the banqueting hall, where we will leave them for the present "tripping the light fantastic toe."

The arrangements made for the comfort of the negro servants, consisted of a sumptuous repast, laid in a temporary out-building, after partaking of which, washed down with heavy libations of the national drink—whiskey, for which the blacks have as great partiality as the red, or indeed the white men, they danced on the green, in the language of one of their own melodious songs, "all night, till the broad day-light."

After a certain time the company dispersed, a portion following the bridal party to Stoney Hill, which became for a season the scene of similar rejoicings, when the bride and groom settled down to the prosaic routine of every-day life on a Virginian plantation.

On the 27th day of April, 1778, the year following the happy event we have just detailed, the bride gave birth to a son, christened John Howe Peyton, who subsequently became one of the most distinguished public men in Virginia, and a brief sketch of whom, in the next chapter, concludes this volume. Of his union with Annie Howe four sons were born.

Eight months after the return of the Howes to Belleville from Jamaica, when it was known that my grandfather had returned from New Mexico, and was Annie Howe's accepted lover, Captain Pelham sold his commission and returned to England, to take possession of a handsome estate, devised him by his maiden aunt, who died suddenly some months previous. Captain Pelham subsequently married in England and removed to Virginia, where he left a numerous offspring. The reader will recall the distinguished career of the lamented Captain Pelham of the Confederate Artillery, and the indomitable pluck and spirit exhibited by him during the American civil war. General (Stonewall) Jackson enthusiastically said of this descendant of the English Pelhams, at the battle of Fredericksburg, when he was holding in an advanced position, 20,000 Federal troops at bay with four guns, " With a Pelham upon either flank and my brigade in the centre, the world could not drive me from my position."

Before closing these pages, it must be mentioned that Mr. Scroggin Jones became a great favourite in the neighbourhood of Belleville, where he was regarded quite as a character. He divided his time between piscatory amusements and the Virginia Court House, though after a long attendance upon the latter, he held the Virginia judges in prodigious contempt. He often said when ridiculing their decisions, "I wonder what 'my lud' or 'his ludship' would say at *that*, or *that*, repeating certain remarks of the Virginia jurists.

"I wonder what you know about law," said one day, a crusty old planter, who didn't relish Jimmy's satire upon the local magistracy, "or as for the matter of that, about fish, except the eating of them, you blown up cockney."

"I beg you," said Mr. Jones, interposing, " to indulge in no intemperate language, no angry declamation, no windy effusions ! Have your own way about planting tobacco, or growing corn, but as to the law, in this presence 'twere better to be silent. Did I not live under the shadow of Westminster over twenty years, and see ' his ludship' go and return from court every day ? Sir, I I don't like to be peremptory, but I must say don't controvert Scoggin Jones on a point of law."

Mr. Jones' heat, and the earnestness with which he defended his dignity in his last stronghold, where he entrenched himself behind Westminster Hall and his 'ludship' was irresistably ludicrous, and whatever irritation his contempt for Virginia justice may have momentarily excited among the cavaliers, all was forgotten in a general burst of laughter, amid loud cries of hear! hear! and cheers.

Twelve months before the wedding, the venerable John Peyton departed this life for a better, full of years and full of honours, at the advanced age of sixty-nine years. He was in many respects a remarkable man, and his family and friends never wearied of speaking of his virtues. Forty years after his death his character was a common theme of conversation in the family circle. The late Right Reverend Bishop of Virginia, who died in 1858, quite four score years of age, has often spoken to the writer of the estimation in which he was held by his own father, who told him that nothing but his want of ability to do justice to the theme, prevented him from attempting a biographical sketch. The Bishop's father said in a note referring to him, it would require no common pencil to depict the undeviating rectitude of his conduct, the unshaken constancy of his friendship, the unwearied activity of his benevolence, and invariable warmth of his affections, the untarnished purity of his habits, and the unabated fervour of his piety. Often has the writer heard him spoken of by those who remembered him, as by Annie Howe, who died at Montgomery Hall, 1833, over eighty years of age, as combining within himself every noble and generous quality, as being the most perfect specimen that could be imagined of the upright man and thorough christian gentleman.

He was for many years a magistrate for the county of Stafford, and sat regularly at the quarter sessions, with great advantage to the public, and with perfect satisfaction to the bar. The acuteness of his intellect, the power of his memory, his devotion to the business of the court, and his anxious desire to do complete justice, were long spoken of in Stafford county with admiration and gratitude. To his family, and all those who shared his private friendship, it was well known that all these qualities were associated with kind feelings, and an affectionate heart.

But it is not the writer's purpose to indulge in any attempt at a description of him. He has heard enough of him from his grandmother, Annie Howe Peyton, and from the late Mrs. Fanny Peyton Brown, widow of Judge John Brown, of the Circuit Superior Court of Virginia, and others, to enable him to say that he was universally known and acknowledged as a man of gifted intellect, and penetrating good sense. He lived, as had his father, Henry Peyton, Esquire, and his grandfather, Benjamin John E., the son of Robert, the first who emigrated from England, in the seclusion of his country estate, devoted to rural life, and the cultivation of social happiness. He took no part in public affairs, further than his duties as magistrate of the county required, and as vestryman of the church. With his friends he enjoyed free intercourse—delighted to be surrounded by his family, and had little taste for public life.

Charles Lucas left a numerous progeny in Virginia. His children's children continue to the present day in the service of my grandfather's descendants. His eldest son,

Charles Lucas, Jun., died in Staunton in 1850, at the age of seventy-five. Obedience, fidelity and industry characterized alike father and son. One of his daughters, Sarah Craig, was the wet-nurse of the writer, and treated him in infancy and manhood with the affection of a mother. This kind and excellent woman died in 1865 from, doubtless, the cruelties, privations and sufferings brought upon the people of Virginia by the occupation of the Federal army.

In conclusion, it remains but to be said that my grandfather never recovered from the effects of his wound. That all his hopes of being able to render active service to his country thus perished, as the bright hopes of man often perish in the bud. In the autumn of 1798, at the early age of forty-five, he expired at Stoney Hill, leaving a wife and six children to mourn his untimely end. The traveller who may now wander in the historic regions of the northern neck of Virginia, where the fiercest battles of the Civil War were fought under Federal and Confederate leaders, and to the quiet dells of Stoney Hill Park, stretching down to the pure waters of the Acquia, glittering in silvery lustre amongst the shadows of many branches and thick foliage, will find the cypress planted by Annie Howe upon the grave of my grandfather, immediately after his death. It was beneath the venerable trees of this enchanting wilderness, which seems more like a forest in a beautiful romance, than a reality, where the beautiful and the vast are blended together, that the wounded officer reposed his withered and broken frame for twenty years.

The friendly visitor to Stoney Hill might often during this period have seen him reposing upon the mossy bank, with no companion but his faithful wife. Here they passed many an afternoon hour in solitude and seclusion, engaged in acts of pious devotion. His reason told him, her penetrating eye saw too clearly the progress of disease, and the inevitably fatal result. He bore the truth with christian fortitude, pious resignation, undisturbed by those guilty agitations of mind, to which the wicked are exposed. Oppressed, almost overcome by her feelings, Annie Howe always demeaned herself in his presence with cheerfulness and composure. It was only when she had assisted him to his fireside seat, and retired to her own chamber, that the troubled sigh issued from her afflicted breast, and the flow of bitter tears descended down her cheeks of sorrow. Under those venerable oaks he sheltered himself during the long period when he was quietly passing away;* and under them he now sleeps the sleep of the just, side by side with his fathers.†

* His gun-shot wound was ascertained to have injured the vertebra, and brought on a disease which proved fatal when he was in his forty-fifth year.

† In the private burial ground of the family at Stoney Hill, are interred side by side,
    Benjamin J. E. Peyton,(a) nascitur 1670, obit 1735.
    Henry Peyton, nascitur 1690, obit 1760.
    John Peyton, nascitur 1710, obit 1777.
    John Rowzée Peyton, nascitur 1751, obit 1798.
Robert Peyton, father of Benjamin, is buried at Isleham, Virginia, and John Howe Peyton, son of John Rowzée, in Trinity Church-yard, Staunton.

(a) B. J. E. Peyton was born in Virginia, but shortly thereafter was

It is impossible to wander over the grassy lawns and through the solemn groves of these lovely grounds, where rare and exotic plants fill the air with their perfume, and flourish in wanton and unpruned luxuriance, while far off stretch the dark forests of oak and pine, without solemn and interesting emotions; to pensively muse, in the deep silence which is still reigning in vale and grove, upon the lives of those who once lived here, and the manners and costumes of other days, without being a better, wiser, and happier man. He who casts his eyes from the portico of the hoary and honoured hall, when the crimson light of a summer's evening, falls upon the scene below, rich in the loveliness of native grace, cannot but praise God, who over land and ocean His blessing hand extends, giving us this green earth, its goodly trees, living waters, and countless blessings, without discovering in the unchangeable nature of these blessings the infinite love of that Almighty Father, who is the same "yesterday, to-day, and for ever."

sent to England for education, where having graduated at Cambridge, he joined the English force in Holland under Marlborough, assisted at the capture of Liege in 1702, and engaged in the battle won by the British Fleet in the West Indies, over the French in 1703. Whilst at Cambridge he made the acquaintance of the Czar, Peter the Great, then (1698) in England, to acquire the art of ship-building, of whose eccentricities and gross habits he related many characteristic anecdotes on his return home, to the scandal of his Virginian relatives, who did not believe the Muscovite Autocrat to be anything but a polished and accomplished gentleman.

A

BIOGRAPHICAL SKETCH

OF

JOHN HOWE PEYTON, ESQ.

OF

MONTGOMERY HALL,

AUGUSTA COUNTY, VIRGINIA.

Gratulor quod cum quem necesse erat diligere, qualiscunque opet, talem habemus, ut libenter quoque deligamus. Cicero.

BIOGRAPHICAL SKETCH

OF

JOHN HOWE PEYTON, ESQ.,

OF

MONTGOMERY HALL, AUGUSTA COUNTY, VIRGINIA.

John Howe Peyton, the eldest son of the union of J. Rowzée Peyton and Annie Howe, was born at Stoney Hill, Stafford County, Virginia, on the 27th day of April 1778. Virginia was then an English colony, but America in the throes of the Revolution, which terminated in her independence at the conclusion of the peace with Great Britain in 1783. Until he attained his sixteenth year he pursued a similar course of education with his father, having been provided at an early period with a tutor. His father, calling to mind his own youthful days, his retired temper, which caused him to take little pleasure in the amusements of his comrades, and his wonderful escape from shipwreck when returning from New York, which had a powerful effect in elevating his disposition and making him seem under the especial care of Providence, entertained on all these accounts, a watchful anxiety for the proper education and personal safety of his son, and exercised great circumspection in the choice of a tutor.

He selected for this position, an English gentleman by the name of Priestley, who was distinguished for profound scholarship and original genius, and who was, therefore, every way adapted to awaken the dormant energies of his pupil. Mr. Priestley's strictly moral life, pious habits, and candid manners gained for him universal esteem. Mr. Peyton, therefore, entrusted his son to his tutelage with confidence, but at the same time kept a watchful eye over the whole of his studies, and the general tenor of his conduct. Not unfrequently he was present during his hours of application, and took infinite pleasure in watching his progress in every branch of knowledge. In every branch also of manly exercise he received instruction, and displayed great delight in them. But though of determined courage, as the lad often showed, and of heroic sentiments, combined with the strictest sense of honour, it was quite obvious before he was sixteen that the silent charms of the Muses had mightier attractions for him, than the rough life of a soldier. Accordingly at sixteen, instead of being placed in a military school, he was sent to Dumfries Academy, which continued in a flourishing condition down to the year 1795. Two years following, he matriculated at the University of New Jersey, Nassau Hall, Princeton, where he was graduated, with double first-class honours, (classics and mathematics), as M.A., in 1799. Immediately thereafter he returned to Stoney Hill, and commenced the study of the law, under the supervision and instruction of General Minor, the leader of the circuit. The year following his father died, and shortly after this sad event, the more readily and successfully to prosecute his legal studies, he repaired to Richmond, and became a pupil of the late Judge Bushrod Washington, one of the associate justices of the Supreme Court of the United States. Within six months of his father's death, he obtained his "licence," and entered upon the practical part of his calling in Fredericksburg, meeting with immediate success, business coming to him from the beginning.

His first speech was made in defence of a gentleman charged with murder. The aggravated nature of the case created great excitement in the community, and was watched with the deepest interest by thousands. The murderer was a gentleman, who had killed a tradesman in hot blood for insultingly demanding a bill under peculiar and mortifying circumstances, when the gentleman was surrounded by company. The case was further embarrassed by the jealousy and ill feeling existing between the different classes. A cry had already been raised that there was no law for the weak and humble, that a poor man having been slaughtered by a gentleman of wealth and position, there was no prospect of his punishment; that the law in Virginia was a net which only caught small flies, and through which " big bugs" forced their way. Such was the exciting language in which the tradespeople spoke of the matter, and the jury in this case was composed chiefly of them. The facts of the rencontre were so clearly proven, and the guilt of the accused was so unmistakeably established, that people wondered what could be said in the defence, even those who sympathized with the prisoner. Mr. Peyton's friends were in despair at his embarrassing position. He was about to make his maiden effort; much was expected of the distinguished collegian, and yet his case was so desperate that it was supposed that the oldest and ablest at the bar could say nothing. Being junior counsel he led off in the defence. Rising in the midst of an intensely excited, but perfectly quiet audience, and commencing with the proposition that a man's honour was dearer than his life, was the "immediate jewel of his soul," and that when assailed in his honour and outraged in his feelings, he was justified in striking down his enemy whoever he might be; that in fact it was but a species of self-defence, he proceeded in a speech so full of novel and startling propositions; sustained by a chain of such ingenious though sophistical reasoning, and the whole so full of fervid eloquence and delivered with such declamatory power, that he completely carried away the court, jury and audience. When he resumed his seat, it was amidst a burst of applause which the presence of the Court could not repress. The senior counsel seized him by the hand, saying "I never heard such a speech in all my experience. You, even you, yourself, could not make it again." Not another word was spoken by counsel, though the States attorney made an effort to be heard, the jury declared that they were satisfied, and pronounced their verdict of *not guilty* from their places in open court. His fame was already established, his fortune made. He left the Courthouse that day, the first day he had entered the arena, with an extraordinary reputation. This auspicious beginning was indeed *le commencement de la fin.*

His intimate friend at this period was a young barrister, William A. G. Dade, a ripe scholar and trained lawyer, who subsequently became a Judge of the Superior Court of Law and Chancery in Virginia. Mr. Dade was related to the family at Stoney Hill, which doubtless increased their intimaey, but it was chiefly the result of their mutual love of letters. Much of their time was passed in each other's society, and they invariably went the circuit together, principally engaged in discussing, not grave matters of the law, but the more congenial subject of the ancient authors, thus enlarging their minds, and refining their tastes.*

Man is not completed in the closet, has been more than once said. Society finishes the work, and gives the ingenious mind all that embellishment and dignity which it is capable of receiving. By intercourse with the learned, the penetrating and the virtuous, our knowledge is arranged, our best powers called forth, and our best habits formed and established. Living examples make a more sensible and durable impression, than those which we receive from books; the soul is apt to grow torpid in seclusion, but in company it is kept in a quick and pleasurable agitation; its fire grows more ardent and pure by mixing with congenial spirits, and it imitates, it emulates

---

* Their intimacy was kept up through life, and many boxes of their letters and papers, which came into the hands of the writer, as executor of his father, John Howe Peyton, and a selection from which he had hoped to give to the public were destroyed during the American Civil War 1861-65.

the greatness which it surveys with admiration. Neither of these young men were ignorant that those advantages result from good connections, and they both early sought the association of the most celebrated for talent and learning.

In 1800 Mr. Peyton, very shortly after entering upon his professional career, won the regards of an amiable and accomplished lady, Susan Madison, daughter and co-heiress of Strother Madison Esq., and niece of the Right Reverend the Bishop Madison of Virginia. By her he left an only child, Colonel William Madison Peyton, of Roanoke, Virginia, for many years a distinguished member of the General Assembly of Virginia, and late Inspector-general of the State, and aid-de-camp to his Excellency the Commander-in-Chief, *Govenor Campbell of Virginia*.

Mr. Peyton was elected from his native county to the Lower House of the Virginian Assembly in 1806, and served till 1810, when he removed from Stafford to the Valley of Virginia, and was no longer eligible. During his legislative career, an exciting controversy arose in the United States upon the subject of a tribunal for settling disputes between the State and Federal Judiciary. Many apprehended that unless some such tribunal was established and it was alleged that there was none under the existing constitution, collisions would occur between the government of the Union, and the State governments, and eventuate in Civil War.

The State of Pennsylvania took action upon the subject, and communicated with the State of Virginia, when it will be seen from the following extracts from the proceedings of the Virginia Assembly, that Mr. Peyton prepared on behalf of Virginia a preamble and resolutions of great ability, which were unanimously passed, and not only put the question to rest as to Virginia and Pennsylvania, but in the whole country.*

---

*Virginia Legislature.
Extract from the message of Governor Tyler of Virginia, December 4th, 1809.

" A proposition from the State of Pennsylvania is herewith submitted, with Governor Snyder's letter enclosing the same, in which is suggested the propriety of amending the Constitution of the United States so as to prevent collision between the Government of the Union and the State Governments.

" House of Delegates, Friday, Dec. 15th, 1809.
" On motion ordered that so much of the Governor's communication as relates to the communication of the Governor of Pennsylvania, on the subject of an amendment, proposed by the legislature of the State to the Constitution of the United States, be referred to Messrs. *Peyton*, Otey, Cabell, Walker, Madison, Holt, Newton, Parker, Stevenson, Randolph, Cocke, Wayatt and Ritchie.

" Thursday, January 11th, 1810.
" Mr. *Peyton*, from the Committee, to whom was referred that part of the Governor's communication which relates to the amendment proposed by the State of Pennsylvania, to the Constitution of the United States, made the following report.

" The Committee to whom was referred the communication of the Governor of Pennsylvania, covering certain resolutions of the Legislature of that State proposing an amendment of the Constitution of the United States by the appointment of an impartial tribunal to decide disputes between the State and Federal Judiciary, have had the same under their consideration, and are of opinion that a tribunal is already provided by the Constitution of the

At this period, his legal reputation had already become so high and extended, that he was invited to accept the

---

United States to wit: the Supreme Court, more eminently qualified from their habits and duties, from the mode of their selection, and from the tenure of their offices, to decide the disputes aforesaid in an enlightened and impartial manner than any other tribunal which could be created.

"The members of the Supreme Court are selected from those in the United States, who are most celebrated for virtue and legal learning, not at the will of a single individual, but by the concurrent wishes of the President and Senate of the United States; they will therefore have no local prejudices or partialities. The duties they have to perform lead them necessarily to the most enlarged and accurate acquaintance with the jurisdiction of the Federal and State Courts together, and with the admirable symmetry of our Government. The tenure of their offices enables them to pronounce the sound and correct opinions they may have formed without fear, favour, or partiality.

"The amendment of the Constitution proposed by Pennsylvania seems to be founded upon the idea that the Federal Judiciary will, from a lust of power, enlarge their jurisdiction, to the total annihilation of the jurisdiction of the State Courts; that they will exercise their will instead of the law and the Constitution.

"This argument if it proves anything, would operate more strongly against the tribunal proposed to be created, which promises so little, than against the State Courts, which, for the reasons given, have everything connected with their appointment calculated to insure confidence. What security have we, were the proposed amendments adopted, that this tribunal would not substitute their will and their pleasure in place of the law? The Judiciary are the weakest of the three departments of government, position of Commonwealth Attorney, or Public Prosecutor, and removed to the county of Augusta, lying in the

---

and least dangerous to the political rights of the constitution; they hold neither the purse nor the sword; and even to enforce their own judgments and decisions, must ultimately depend upon the executive arm. Should the Federal judiciary, however unmindful of their weakness, unmindful of the duty which they owe to themselves, and their country, become corrupt and transcend the limits of their jurisdiction, would the proposed amendment oppose even a probable barrier to such an improbable state of things?

"The creation of a tribunal, such as is proposed by Pennsylvania, so far as we are able to form an idea of it, from the description given in the resolutions of the Legislature of the State, would, in the opinion of your Committee, tend rather to invite than to prevent collisions between the Federal and State Courts. It might also become in process of time, a serious and dangerous embarrassment to the operations of the general Government.

"Resolved, therefore: That the Legislature of this State do disapprove of the amendment to the Constitution of the United States proposed by the Legislature of Pennsylvania.

"Resolved also: That his Excellency the Governor be and he is hereby requested to transmit forthwith a copy of the foregoing preamble and resolutions to each of the Senators and representatives of this State in Congress, and to the executives of the several States in the Union, with a request that the same be laid before the Legislatures thereof.

"The said Resolutions being read a second time, were, on motion, ordered to be referred to a Committee of the whole House on the State of the Commonwealth.

"Tuesday, January 23rd, 1810.

"The House according to the order of the day, resolved

heart of the beautiful valley of the Shenandoah. Here he purchased an estate called "Montgomery Hall," situated

---

itself into a Committee of the whole house on the state of the Commonwealth, and after some time spent therein, Mr. Speaker resumed the chair, and Mr. Stannard of Spottsylvania, reported that the Committee had, according to order, had under consideration the preamble and resolution of the Select Committee, to whom was referred that part of the Governor's communication which relates to the amendment proposed to the Constitution of the United States by the Legislature of Pennsylvania, had gone through with the same, and directed him to report them to the House without amendment, which he handed in to the clerk's table.

"And the question being put, on agreeing to the said preamble and resolutions, they were agreed to by the House unanimously.

"Ordered that the clerk carry the said preamble and resolutions to the Senate, and desire their concurrence.

In Senate.

"Wednesday, January 24th, 1810,

"The preamble and resolutions on the amendment to the Constitution of the United States, proposed by the Legislature of Pennsylvania by the appointment of an impartial tribunal to decide disputes between the State and Federal judiciary, being also delivered in and twice read, on motion was ordered to be committed to Messieurs Nelson, Currie, Campbell, Upshur and Wolfe.

"Friday, January 26th, 1810.

"Mr. Nelson reported from the Committee on the preamble and resolutions on the Amendment, proposed by the Legislature of Pennsylvania, &c., &c., that the Committee had, according to order, taken the said preamble and resolutions under their consideration, and directed him to report them without any amendment.

near the town of Staunton, and this was ever afterwards his place of residence.

Notwithstanding his large practice, and the zeal with which he engaged in the avocations of civil life, he was not unmindful of other duties which sometimes devolve in a country without powerful neighbours, or a standing army, as were the United States previous to 1861, upon the peaceful citizen. During the year 1812, when the second war occurred between Great Britain and the United States, and Richmond was threatened by a powerful British force, Mr. Peyton immediately volunteered his services, and was appointed Chief of Staff to Major-General Robert Porterfield. He entered at once upon his duties, marched to Richmond, and served with credit till the close of the war in 1814. The war over, he returned to private life, and to the practice of his profession, and was immediately appointed by the Hon. William Wirt, Attorney-General of the United States, Assistant United States District Attorney for Virginia. From this period till 1836, he gave his entire energies to the profession, acquiring great distinction, and a large fortune. During this period, the distinguishing peculiarities of his intellect made themselves more manifest. It was observed that in all of his investigations, his philosophical mind rose above the technicalities of the system of the common law, to the consideration of general principles, and he was never more eloquent than when expatiating upon those great principles

---

"And on the question being put, thereupon the same was agreed to unanimously."

which lie at the foundation of all duty, and are equally applicable to all its forms.

In 1820 death deprived him of his wife, Susan Madison, who had been for many years a confirmed invalid. In 1822 he married his second wife. The object of his present choice was Ann Montgomery Lewis, daughter of Major John Lewis, of the Sweet Springs, a noted Revolutionary officer, and personal friend of Washington. Major Lewis, like his father, Colonel William Lewis, and his uncle, General Andrew Lewis, served in the Indian wars which preceded the American Revolution, and in the War of Independance, having been present in almost all the battles of that fratricidal strife which occurred in the Northern Colonies.* To her warm affection, which was displayed in the care of his orphan son, and as the companion of his long life, and the mother of a rising family, he owed for many years that domestic happiness which was the chief solace of his life, and from which he allowed no public honours to wholly withdraw him. From the period of his second marriage, his life passed on in a course of uninterrupted happiness down to the hour of his death.

In 1836 he was elected a Virginia Senator, and served in this capacity till 1845, when he resigned on account of declining health. He was elected to the Senate against his wishes, and to the no small detriment of his private interest. To accept this unprofitable employment, he was

---

* In 1830 the Government of the United States made a special grant of 13,000 acres of public land to the heirs of my maternal grandfather, Major Lewis, in consideration of his distinguished services in the Revolutionary War.

required by the constitution of the State to relinquish the lucrative office of public prosecutor. The people invested him with the senatorial robes under circumstances eminently calculated to gratify his pride. Though making no scruples of his disinclination to serve, he was elected by a large majority, over a well-known public man, Mr. Robert S. Brooks, who had in various situations done the State good service.

At the expiration of his first term of service he wished to retire, but an ill-timed opposition, under peculiar circumstances, caused him to reappear as a candidate. The writer will be pardoned for alluding, at this point, to the circumstances under which an opposition was now raised to Mr. Peyton, as it enables him to give an amusing illustration of his pleasantry, and the effect with which he used the power of ridicule.

During the last session of his first senatorial term, a bill was introduced into the Assembly for raising the taxes to meet the interest on a largely increased public debt, resulting from the extension of the internal improvement system of the State. This was an exceedingly unpopular measure with the people—as what tax bill is not ?—who declared that the improvements were unnecessary ; that if necessary, they would pay, and if this were true, they would be constructed by private companies. That it was bad policy in the Assembly to have inaugurated such a system, and ruinous to the interests of the people ; and they declared, most unmistakeably, their purpose to return a new set of representatives opposed to their measures.

Three or four cunning lawyers, who had long wished to enter public life, thought they now saw a favourable opportunity, and a ticket was formed to oppose Mr. Peyton's re-election to the Senate, and that of the three members to the Lower House. An active canvas commenced, the four new candidates meeting the old members upon the hustings, save Mr. Peyton, who declined engaging in the canvas; intimating, however, that he would speak at any mass meeting of the people which should occur at the county towns, while he was travelling the circuit.

He came to Lexington in 1842 while the Author was a cadet in the Military Academy, to attend the session of the Rockbridge term of the Superior Court, and a grand mass meeting of the people was called to take place at this time, that the candidates might have an opportunity of addressing them. There was great excitement, and to enable the cadets to hear the discussion, a holiday was granted to all but the guard on duty.

Among others, the Author attended. The three members of the Lower House made long, grave and able arguments in vindication of their course in voting an increase of the taxes, and to shelter themselves behind Mr. Peyton, declared that in pursuing this course, they had but followed the advice and pursued the course of their—the people's—honoured Senator. When they had concluded, their legal opponents replied in equally grave speeches, artfully conceived so as to pander to the passions of the people. They concluded their addresses by promising the people generally, that if elected, they would vote "for giving everything to everybody."

Mr. Peyton now rose to address the assemblage, and remarked, that it was true he had voted for increased taxation, and his confidence was perfect that in endeavouring by this course to preserve the honour and reputation of the people of Virginia, he should receive their approbation and support, notwithstanding the present clamour. He said taxes were notoriously distasteful, and it was always a delicate matter to increase them, and therefore it was not unnatural that some dissatisfaction was felt, and some opposition expressed to their course; but (turning to the three lawyers by whom the old ticket was opposed), he said, least of all did he expect opposition from the legal fraternity, for while it was true that he had voted to lay a tax of ten dollars a head upon lawyers, in the preceding clause he had voted to levy a tax of double upon jackasses!

The ludicrous manner and peculiar emphasis with which he uttered this remark, convulsed the audience with laughter and applause. Cheer after cheer now arose in favour of the old ticket, and groan after groan was uttered for the new. In a moment all the laboured arguments of the old and new candidates were forgotten. In a single sentence he had swept everything before him. The chagrined members of the opposition assumed in turn all the glowing colours of the expiring dolphin. When quiet was restored, he proceeded in fifteen minutes to explain in a lucid and conclusive manner the necessity for increased taxation, and appealing in a strain of fervid eloquence, in conclusion, to their pride as men, their pride as freemen, and their pride as Virginians, to uphold her honour, he resumed his seat, amidst immense and long-continued applause. Next day the walls were placarded with great bills. " Vote for Peyton and paying your debts—vote for the old ticket." " No one objects to being taxed, but lawyers and jackasses."

It need scarcely be said, he was returned by a triumphant majority.

Mr. Peyton's great majority was a tribute to his abilities and his capacity for public usefulness—nothing more. He was never a popular man, or people's favourite—was not unfrequently styled an *aristocrat*, and was, as everybody knew, the furthest possible removed from that class of degraded demagogues, who are politely known in America as " popular men," " the people's favourites." These are the mild terms used to designate those selfish demagogues, who hover about county court-houses, often calling themselves attorneys, battening upon the strifes of the community, and ready to pander to the vilest passions of the people to secure a seat in the legislature, in a State convention, in a college directory, in a railway board, in any place indeed, where there is a small per diem and a prospect of jobbery. Proudly conscious of his own rectitude and his intellectual superiority, he disdained the society of these tricksters, detesting them as thoroughly as their vices. He was a terror too to these harpies. There was a fire in his eye, a punishing glance that prostrated these creatures, so that the words of Scripture might be applied to him: " The King, when he sits upon the throne of His Majesty, chases by a glance of his countenance every evil thing;" whilst in the thunder of his voice there was such force, that it struck to the earth whomsoever he addressed in anger. Hence, he was not what is called in America a popular man—or a favourite with the masses. Could scarcely be so characterized, while the jackalls and whippers in of party where whining at his heels. Nor was he at all conciliating in his manners, but it must be acknowledged, was a man of extraordinary pride—a pride which indeed pervaded the whole man. As Macaulay once said of the Prime Minister, William Pitt, pride was written in the rigid lines of his face, was marked by the way in which he walked, in which he sate, in which he stood, and above all in which he bowed. Such pride, of course, inflicted many wounds. He was popular, however, in the highest and best sense of that term, being a great favourite with those whose good opinion was worth possessing. There was so much childlike simplicity, mixed with the severity of his deportment, that he filled all at the same time with veneration and love. This was so marked, that the good whom he sometimes severely reproved for their shortcomings, and thereby provoked were amongst his most faithful adherents, and his enemies were so profoundly impressed with his integrity, that though occasionally holding no personal intercourse with him, they sought his aid and counsel when in trial and tribulation. This was remarkably illustrated and exquisitely proved by the act of John Churchman, Esq., of Augusta, Virginia, formerly High Sheriff of the county. Mr. Churchman was so incensed by one of Mr. Peyton's reprimands, that all intercourse between them ceased. Some years later, the former High Sheriff was involved in a law suit of an important and harrassing character, and he applied, through a mutual friend, to Mr. Peyton for his professional assistance, which was given to him freely and successfully.

The limits of this sketch will not permit us to follow him year by year, through the course of his long and useful life. During the time when he represented the public in the Senate and Legislature, it was to the entire satisfaction of his constituents and with great and acknowledged advantage to the legislation and jurisprudence of the State. Though he retired from the Legislature in 1810, and refused to serve longer in that capacity or in Congress, though often solicited to do so, (such were the demands made upon his time by his increased practice); his advice was often sought upon occasions of great public interest, and there were few measures, State or National, which did not derive some assistance from his powerful intellect and extensive information. Such was his modesty, that through life he neither sought nor desired notoriety, and was content without display, or reward, to contribute all he had to the promotion of the public good.

But it was not only as a public man, an eminent lawyer and a distinguished statesman, that he was known and respected. In private life, and it is necessary to consider him in this light in order to do justice to his character—he inspired affectionate reverence, by reason of his loving and generous spirit. His charity was boundless, embracing all relations and friends, and indeed common humanity. In his intercourse with his family, he was not only tender and affectionate but sportive and familiar, though this latter quality was tempered by a gentle dignity which restrained insensibly the exuberance of youthful spirits within just bounds.

This sketch might be considered incomplete without some notice of his religious sentiments. Piety and morality dictated the whole course of his life, and several years before his death, which occurred April 3rd, 1847, at his home, in Augusta, he openly professed his faith in the religion of Jesus Christ, and united himself with the Protestant Episcopal Church, thus adding his solemn testimony of belief to the practical illustrations afforded by his life. No words of our's can so well express what we feel, as the solemn and beautiful thoughts embraced in the following lines, and which are worthy of application here.

> "Peace to the just man's memory;—let it grow
> Greener with years, and blossom through the flight
> Of ages; let the mimic leaves show
> His calm benevolent features; let the light
> Stream on his deeds of love, that shunned the sight
> Of all but Heaven; and in the books of fame
> The glorious record of his virtues write,
> And hold it up to men, and bid them claim
> A palm like his, and catch from him the hallowed flame."

As we have said, he retired in 1845 to the seclusion of his estate, (Montgomery Hall), where he died from apoplexy two years later. In the "Southern Literary Messenger" for 1850, the following brief sketch of Mr. Peyton appeared. It is from the pen of a worthy and excellent gentleman, Major John Preston, professor of modern languages in the Virginia Military Institute

Lexington. Major Preston, was, however, so much Mr. Peyton's junior, that he only knew him in his declining years, and does but scant justice to the extraordinary merits of the foremost man in his day of the profession in Virginia. Mr. Peyton's youngest brother, Colonel Rowzée Peyton of Geneva, New York,* whose death, (at 82 years of age), occurred October 10th, 1867, and intelligence of which reached London since this work went to press, expressed his surprise and mortification to the writer in 1851, that a notice doing his lamented brother

* Colonel Rowzée Peyton married his second wife, Eliza Murray, in New York city. She was daughter of one of the principal merchants of the place, and connected with many of the most ancient families of that State, but having been born and reared in a non-slave-holding community, she could not reconcile it with her feelings on her conscience to reside in Virginia. Shortly after their marriage, through her influence, Colonel Peyton removed from his native State and became a citizen of New York. If his wife had known something of the futile efforts to naturalize the native American Negro in Africa, and of the untold misery which has since been brought upon them by their forcible emancipation, she would probably have felt less uneasiness in her southern residence. In 1830, Mr. Howe Peyton despatched fifty slaves from the "Wilderness plantation" in Bath County to Liberia. Slaves liberated upon the express condition that they should remove to that colony. They were supplied with suitable clothing, food, &c., and money to cover their expenses for twelve months after their arrival. Mr. Peyton accompanied them in person to Norfolk, and saw them comfortably established on ship board. They had a short and prosperous voyage, and all arrived safe and well in Africa. For two years they wrote regularly, at the end of which time thirty-four had died from dissipation and the effects of the climate. The remaining sixteen were scattered, some relapsing into barbarism, and the others into poverty. For thirty-five years nothing has been heard of them, and all are presumed to have perished. Such are some of the bitter fruits of African Colonization.

so little justice should have been published. It was written with the best motives, however, and was sent to the magazine to be printed by Major Preston without having been exhibited to any member of the Peyton family. Meagre and faint as it is, it will serve though imperfectly and indistinctly to present one view of his character, and is accordingly included herein, without change or modification. It may be doubted, however, whether any benefit has accrued to Mr. Peyton's fame from the unsafe sort of embalmment it has received in the sketch of the well-meaning Major Preston.

It has always been a source of great regret to the Author that he was too young to hear many, or understand any of his father's speeches made when he was in his prime. He has often stood in a crowded assembly, when a boy, and seen the audience swayed to and fro by his eloquence, at one moment convulsed with laughter, and at another drowned in tears, without being able to follow his argument or to appreciate his eloquence, save by his splendid manner and the wonderful effect his words produced.

It may not be uninteresting, if he pauses here to mention the only occasion, after he attained manhood, on which he heard his father speak, and when he spoke, as he had never heard man speak before.

On the completion of the Author's university career in 1844, he returned to "Montgomery Hall," when his father was in his 67th year, and after he had been prostrated by an attack of apoplexy, accompanied with paralysis of his left side, and from which he had only partially recovered.

At this period Mr. Peyton had retired from the bar, but shortly after, an important case in which he had been previously engaged by an old friend, James A. McCue Esq., came on for trial. Mr. McCue was deeply interested in this cause, and appealed to Mr. Peyton as a personal friend, to give him the benefit of his legal knowledge and experience. Mr. Peyton resisted this application for some time, pleading his age and infirmities. Mr. McCue, however, was so deeply interested in the matter and urged with so much earnestness and feeling his claims upon him as an old friend, that he finally yielded to his solicitations. The day the cause was to be argued the writer accompanied his father to the Court-house without any special interest in this case, but anxious to hear one of his arguments even at this advanced period of his life, and also apprehensive lest the excitement of the cause might prostrate him in his then delicate health, and that his assistance might be required. When he entered the Court a cause was in progress which occupied about an hour. At the end of his time the case of McCue and Ralston was called. Mr. Ralston's senior counsel, the Hon. Alexander H. H. Stuart a distinguished jurist and accomplished gentleman was absent. His associate counsel, a young attorney, rose and said, "that he had fully investigated the case and that it was so plainly and palpably in favour of his client (Mr. Ralston), that he did not know how to proceed to make it clearer, that he felt a curiosity to know what could be said upon the other side, and he added somewhat presumptuously, that he was considered to have a fair share of imagination, and quite as much penetration as ordinary men, and yet he really could not comprehend how the learned counsel on the other side would proceed to argue against Mr. Ralston such a case." After this fashion the young attorney proceeded for thirty minutes, resuming his seat with quite a triumphant air and without having adduced a solitary argument upon a single point, because as he alleged, " no lawyer could find one in support of a case which on its face was so manifestly for his client."

Mr. Peyton then rose feebly from his seat, holding his brief in one hand and supporting himself upon the other which rested on a table, and without taking any notice whatever of what the young man had said, or even looking at, or in the slightest manner referring to him, proceeded in a coloquial style to argue his cause, in a speech of such perspicacity, force and beauty, that it rivetted the attention of every one in the house. All were led on, irresistably fascinated by the grace of his diction and the clearness of his demonstration. At the end of twenty-five minutes when he concluded, the audience seemed to awake from a spell-bound condition, from a delightful intellectual trance. The writer comprehended then for the first time in his life the irresistable power of simple eloquence, and left the Court-house more delighted than he had ever risen from a demonstration in Euclid, or the solution of any problem in mathematics, and understanding the grounds of his father's wonderful success and great and extended reputation.

An appeal was subsequently taken from the decision of the lower court in the case. It need scarcely be said, however, that it was decided after Mr. Peyton's death in the Court of Appeals of Virginia upon, and, in accordance with the principles laid down in his speech that day.*

* This cause is reported by Robinson or Grattan.

SKETCH

OF A DISTINGUISHED LAWYER.

The late John H. Peyton Esq., of Staunton, Virginia, was one of the finest specimens that we have ever known of the *complete lawyer*. In Middle and Western Virginia, he was confessedly in the front rank of legal men, and according to the opinions of many, he was first in that rank. During the prime of life, he pursued his profession with a laborious assiduity rarely equalled, and though as age advanced upon him he remitted his efforts, he did not discontinue his practice until a short time before his death, which occurred April 3rd, 1847, in the 69th year of his age. None of his contemporaries secured a more ample reward, in either reputation or pecuniary emolument.

We have spoken of Mr. Peyton as a complete lawyer. Law, as a practical profession, has several departments, and it is not unusual to see a lawyer distinguished in some of them, with a compensating deficiency in others. Some practitioners are successful collectors—some are much esteemed as judicious advisers in matters not strictly legal—some are favourite advocates, with a sub-division into those who are influential with the Court, and those who are persuasive before a jury—some are designated good judges of law, or, in other words, safe counsellors, and of some the *forte* is Common Law Practice, while others are distinguished as Chancery lawyers. The organization of the courts in Virginia, and the nature of the business, at least in the interior, requires every lawyer to enter upon the whole of this miscellaneous practice; and it is not to be wondered at, that some, even good lawyers, are not equally strong in every part. Mr. Peyton knew every part of his profession thoroughly. He had studied diligently as a student, he had known the expectant struggles of the young practitioner; he had practised under the old system before the reorganization of the judiciary, and afterwards under the new; he had met in contest the strongest men in each department of the profession, and he had made himself a champion in all. We may add that some lawyers who exhibit the highest skill in securing the rights of their clients, are foolishly ignorant of their own; in other words, they let slip the fair, well-earned profits of their profession—not so with Mr. Peyton. He knew the value of his professional services; he gave them to the fullest extent to those who applied for them, and then he insisted upon just remuneration. We notice this point, not at random, but to present a feature belonging to the character of the complete lawyer.

The characteristic of Mr. Peyton's life was efficiency. This efficiency had for its elements, native vigour of intellect, great resoluteness of character, and courageous self-confidence, ample and thorough acquirements, and the quickness, precision and dexterity of action that belong only to those who have been taught by a varied experience to understand thoroughly human nature. In conversation, Mr. Peyton was ready, entertaining and instructive. But conversation was not his *forte*, though he was fond of it. He was not fluent;. his manner was sometimes too direct for the highest style of polished social intercourse of a general nature, and besides he had a remarkable way of indulging in a strain of covert satirical banter, when his words would be so much at variance with the expression of his countenance, and particularly with the expression of his mouth, that the hearer was often in an uncomfortable state of uncertainty how to take him. His person was large, and his bearing dignified but not graceful. His manner was unaffected, but not without formality, nor was it perfectly conciliatory. Some styled him aristócratic, while none could deny that his self-respect and confident energy gave an imperious cast to his demeanour. We have oftener than once thought applicable to him, in a general way, those lines of Terence.

"Ellum, confidens, catus,
Cum faciem videas, videtur esse quantivis preti,
Tristis severitas inest in voltu, atque in verbis fides."

His voice was true and clear, and capable of sufficient variety, but without a single musical intonation, and a little sharper than you would expect to hear from a man of his size and form. If it is asked what was the style of his speaking, it may be replied—just what might be expected to belong to such a man as has here been described, that is to say, never was the speaker a more complete reflection of the man than in his case. We cannot believe that any one who knew him was ever surprised when they heard him speak—what he said, was just what they would expect him to say. This is often the case with speakers and writers, but not always. Energy, reality and efficiency were his characteristics as a man, and equally so as a speaker. Distinctness of conception lay at the foundation of his excellence. Some great speakers, some even pre-eminently great speakers, not unfrequently hurl unforged thunderbolts. They feel the maddening impulse of the God, but give forth their utterances before the true prophetic fury comes on.

Mr. Peyton's mind was no sybil's cave, whence came forth wind-driven leaves inscribed with mighty thoughts disposed by chance, but a spacious castle, from whose wide open portal issued men at arms, orderly arrayed. He had hardly opened his case, when the hearer was aware that he had thought over the whole of it, had a given course to pursue, and would close when he came to the end of it. This distinctness of conception comprehended the subject as a whole, and shed its light upon each detail belonging to it. This ensured the most perfect method in all that he said. Before he began to speak, he had determined in his own mind, not only the order of the different parts of his discourse, but also their relative importance in producing the general impression. Hence, he was never led away by the tempting character of any peculiar topic, to expatiate upon it unduly; he did not take up matter irrelevant to the case because it might touch himself personally; he never spoke for those behind the bar, nor did he neglect to secure the fruits of victory, in order to pursue an adversary to utter discomfiture. He spoke as a lawyer, he spoke for the verdict, and expected to gain it, by showing that he was entitled to it. Some speakers hope to accomplish their object by single, or at least, successive impulses—now a clinching argumentative question, now a burst of brilliant declamation, and now a piece of keen wit, or a rough personality. Such speakers forget, or do not know that a jury may admire, may be diverted, and even moved, without being won. He that gains the verdict must mould, and sway, and lead, and this is to be effected by continued persistent pressure, rather than by *tours de force*. This Mr. Peyton knew well, and he observed it with perfect self-command. His hearers came away satisfied with the whole, rather than treasuring up remarkable points and passages. Let it not be supposed, however, that he was a cold speaker, who treated men as mere intellectual machines, to be set in motion by the pulleys, screws, and levers of logic. Far from it; he understood human nature well, and knew the motive power of the feelings; but then he knew, too, that the way to excite the most effective sympathy is not to make a loud outcry, but to make a forcible exhibition of real suffering—that the best way to rouse our indignation against fraud, deceit, or oppression, is not to exhort us to hate it, but to show its hatefulness. One of his most distinguished cotemporaries upon the same circuit (still living), was celebrated for his powers as a criminal advocate; his manner was obviously upon the pathetic order, and perhaps a trifle too declamatory. We have seen them in the same cause, and have thought that if the eloquence of Gen. B. flushed the countenance quicker, the earnestness of Mr. Peyton stirred the heart deeper. Of the oratory of a class of speakers by no means rare (not, however, including in this class the distinguished jurist above alluded to), it has been well said that: "declamation roars while passion sleeps;" of speaking justly characterized by this line, Mr. Peyton's was the precise reverse. With him, thought became passionate before the expression became glowing, as the wave swells, before it crests itself with foam.

Mr. Peyton's language was forcible, pure, and idiomatic. It served well as the vehicle of his thoughts, but contributed nothing to them. There is a real and legitimate advantage belonging to the masterly use of words, of which many great speakers know well how to avail themselves.

Mr. Peyton attempted nothing of the sort. His diction was thoroughly English, with a marked preference for the Anglo-Saxon branch of the language, and his sentences came out in the most natural order with unusual clearness and vigour, but not unfrequently with a plainness that bordered upon homeliness. His style, however, was always that of speaking as distinguished from mere conversation—a distinction which some of our modern speakers forget, when in order to appear at their ease, they treat with no little disregard not only the rules of rhetoric, but the rules of grammar as well, and use words and phrases which are (to take a word from the vocabulary we are condemning) nothing better than slang. On the contrary, there was in Mr. Peyton's style the fruit of early studies and high-bred association, a classical tinge, extremely pleasant to the scholar, though perhaps not appreciable by those for whom he generally spoke. It must not be supposed, from what has been said of his excellent method, that he resembled in this respect some of our able but greatly tedious lawyers, who take up in regular succession every possible point in the case, however minute, and worry us by officiously offering help where none is needed —so far from it, he showed his consummate skill as well in what he omitted as in what he handled, and as a general thing, his speeches were shorter in duration, and yet fuller of matter than those of his opponent. His use of figurative language was easy and natural, and not stinted; but his figures were always introduced as illustrations, and not as arguments.

It is not unusual to see a speaker who is unable to enounce distinctly the general principle he wishes to use, throw out an illustration to enable himself to pick out the principle from it, or at least to give his hearers a chance to do it for themselves; not so with Mr. Peyton. He held up the torch of illustration, not to throw a light forward to guide himself in his own investigations, but to enable those following the more readily to tread the road along with him. He had a very noticeable fondness for recurring to the primary fundamental principles of morals, and doubtless he was restrained, by his practical judiciousness, from indulging this disposition to the full. One of his favourite books was Lord Bacon's Essays, and under other circumstances, he might himself have been a distinguished moral essayist.

As may well be supposed, his general strain was grave. The high idea he entertained of the dignity of his profession, and the earnestness with which he gave himself to it, alike precluded either levity or carelessness. However, he was fully able, and quite ready upon occasion, to avail himself of a keen wit, that was all the more effective because it was dry and sarcastic. It occurs to us to mention an instance well known to his circuit, not illustrative of his severity, but of his pleasantry. In a criminal prosecution, he, as prosecuting attorney, was opposed by two gentlemen of ability, whose pathos had been so great as to draw abundant tears from their own eyes. One of them, a gentleman now occupying a distinguished national position, (Honourable Alexander H. H. Stuart, Secretary of the Interior of the Government of the United States,) was noted for the facility with which he could cover over his brilliant eloquence with the liquid varnish of his tears. On this occasion he had been singularly lachrymose, and supported by his colleague in the same way, the sensation produced was very considerable. Mr. Peyton commenced his reply by regretting the disadvantage the commonwealth laboured under, in being represented by him who was a very poor hand at crying, and certainly was not able to cry against two at a time. The ludicrousness of the expression completely neutralized the pathos of his opponents. He was not averse either to a bit of farce now and then, as is shown by the following story told of him. In a remote part of the circuit, a lawyer wished to adorn a moving passage of a speech he was just rising to make, with an apposite example, and applied to Mr. Peyton, sitting beside of him, to help him to the name of the man in the *Bible*, who would have his pound of flesh. With imperturbable gravity he answered *Absolom!* The effect of this confounding Shakespeare and Scripture may be imagined.

We have said that Mr. Peyton was thoroughly furnished in every part of his profession—in one department his qualifications were peculiar and unsurpassed. Without disparagement of others, it may be said, we think, that he was the best Commonwealth's Attorney in the State of Virginia. He was the lawyer of the Commonwealth, and he treated the Commonwealth as a client, and laboured for her with the same industry, zeal, and fidelity that he manifested in behalf of any other client. The oft quoted merciful maxim of the Common Law, "better that ninety and nine guilty men should escape, than one innocent man should suffer," he interpreted as a caution to respect the rights of the innocent, and not as an injunction to clear the guilty, and he laboured to reduce the per centage of rogues unwhipt of justice, as low as possible. With a clearness and force rarely equalled, would he point out the necessity of punishing the guilty, in order that the innocent might be safe, thus exhibiting the absolute consistency of strict justice with true mercy. So simply and earnestly would he do this, that he not only bound the consciences of the jury, but also made them feel that they were individually interested in the faithful execution of the laws. Here his clear perception of the moral principles upon which rests the penal code, and his fondness for recurring to general principles stood him in great stead. It was delightful to hear him expatiate upon this theme, for upon no other was he more truly eloquent.

Mr. Peyton served at different times in both branches of the Legislature, but we speak not of him as a politician. Our purpose has been solely to exhibit some of the qualities which made him an eminent member and ornament of the legal profession.

This is the only record to be found in the vast collection of the British Museum of the life and reputation of one who, for near a half century, filled so deservedly high and conspicuous a place in the public eye of Virginia. In the numerous volumes of the Virginia Common Law and Equity reports in the Museum Library, the heads—it is true—of his arguments, throughout his professional career in the Virginian Court of Appeals, are preserved, but this is all. A curious book might be written on the reputation of lawyers. Occupying often the highest position, and wielding the greatest influence in their day; their ashes are no sooner consigned to the dust than they are comparatively forgotten, certainly by the general public. Every one knows that fortune is inconstant, what could better illustrate that reputation is a bubble?

NARRATIVE

OF THE

CIRCUMSTANCES CONNECTED

WITH THE

SETTLEMENT

OF

JOHN LEWIS

AND

HIS FAMILY IN VIRGINIA.

NARRATIVE

OF THE

CIRCUMSTANCES CONNECTED WITH THE SETTLEMENT OF

M. JEAN LOUIS, OR JOHN LEWIS,

AND HIS FAMILY IN VIRGINIA.

As the Lewis family are repeatedly referred to in the foregoing work, and is one indeed which has performed much distinguished service to the State, a brief account of the peculiar circumstances under which the first settler in America, John Lewis, emigrated to Virginia will not be out of place here.

M. Jean Louis, or John Lewis, was a native and citizen of Ireland, descended from a family of Huguenots, who took refuge in the Kingdom of Great Britain from the persecutions that followed the assassination of Henry IV. of France. The Lewis' first settled in Scotland and afterwards passed into Ireland. His rank was that of an Esquire, and he inherited a handsome estate, which he increased by industry and frugality, until he became lessee of a contiguous property of considerable value. He married in

This sketch is a reprint from "Howe's history of Virginia" to which work it was a contribution from the authors (J.L. Peyton's) family. A sketch more in detail of John Lewis will be found in the "Virginia Historical Register" 1850-1855, also of his Sons in the "new american Cyclopedia" of D. Appleton — also in a work entitled "warfare" by   & in Dr. Willis de Hass' work on Virginia

Scotland where he had gone for education, Margaret Lynn, daughter of the laird of Loch Lynn, who was a descendant of the chieftains of a once powerful clan in the Scottish Highlands. By this marriage he had four sons, three of them, Thomas, Andrew and William born in Ireland, and Charles, the child of his old age, born in Virginia a few months after their settlement in their mountain home.

The emigration of John Lewis to Virginia, was the result of one of those bloody affrays, which at that time so often occurred to disturb the repose, and destroy the happiness of Irish families. The owner of the fee, out of which the leasehold of Lewis was carved, a nobleman of profligate habits and ungovernable passions, seeing the prosperity of his lessee, and repenting the bargain he had concluded, under pretence of entering for an alleged breach of condition, attempted, by the aid of a band of ruffians hired for his purpose, to take forcible possession of his premises. For this end, he surrounded the house with his ruffian band, and called upon Lewis to evacuate the premises without delay, a demand which was instantly and indignantly refused by Lewis; though surprised with a sick brother, his wife, and three young children in the house, and no aid but such as could be afforded by a few faithful domestics, some of whom were French. With this small force, scarce equal to one fourth the number of his assailants, he resolved to maintain his legal rights at every hazard. The enraged nobleman commenced the affray by discharging a fowling piece into the house, by which the invalid brother of Lewis was killed, and Margaret Lynn his wife severely wounded. Upon this, the enraged husband and brother-in-law, Lynn, rushed from the house, attended by their devoted little band of Scotch and French, and soon succeeded in dispersing the assailants, though not until the noble author of the mischief, as well as his bailiff and steward, had perished. By this time the family were surrounded by sympathizing friends and neighbours, from among the Scotch settlers in this part (Province of Ulster) of Ireland, who, after bestowing every aid in their power, advised Lewis to leave the country—a measure rendered necessary by the aristocratic position and family wealth and influence of the late nobleman, and the want of disinterested evidence by which he could establish the facts of the case in his vindication. He, therefore, after drawing up a detailed statement of the affair, which he directed to the proper authorities, embarked on board a vessel bound for America, attended by his family, and a band of about thirty of his faithful tenantry. In due time the emigrants landed on the shores of Virginia and fixed their residence amid the till then unbroken forests of West Augusta. John Lewis' settlement was a few miles below the site of the town of Staunton, on the banks of the stream which bears his name. It may be proper to remark here, that when the circumstances of the affray became known, after due investigation, a pardon was granted to Lewis, and patents are extant in Virginia, by which His Majesty George I. granted to him a large portion of the fair domain of Western Virginia.

For many years after the settlement at Fort Lewis, great amity and good will existed between the neighbouring Indians and the white settlers, whose numbers increased apace, until they became quite a formidable colony. It was then that the jealousy of their Red neighbours became aroused, and a war broke out, which, for cool though desperate courage and activity on part of the whites, and ferocity, cunning, and barbarity on part of the Indians, was never equalled in any age or country.

John Lewis was by this time well stricken in years, but his four sons, who were now grown up, were well qualified to fill his place, and to act the part of leaders to the gallant little band who so nobly battled for the protection of their homes and families. It is not my purpose to go into the details of a warfare, during which scarcely a settlement was exempt from weekly attacks of the savages, and during which the young Lewis' are said never to have spent one month at a time out of active and arduous service. They were the heroes of many a gallant exploit, which are still treasured in the memories of the descendants of the border riflemen, and there are few families among the Alleghanies where the name and deeds of the Lewis' are not familiar as household words.

On one occasion Charles Lewis,* the youngest brother, was captured by the Indians while on a hunting excursion, and after having travelled two hundred miles, barefoot, his arms pinioned behind him, goaded on by the knives of his remorseless captors, he effected his escape. While travelling along the bank of a precipice some twenty feet in height, he suddenly, by a strong muscular exertion, burst the cords which bound him, and plunged down the

* Afterwards Colonel Charles Lewis who was killed at the battle of Point Pleasants.

steep into the bed of a mountain torrent. His persecutors hesitated to follow. In a race of several hundred yards, Lewis had gained slowly upon his pursuers; when, leaping a prostrate tree which lay across his course, his strength suddenly failed, and he fell prostrate and exhausted among the weeds which had grown up in great luxuriance around the body of the tree. Three of the Indians sprang over the tree within a few feet of where their prey lay concealed; but with a feeling of the most devout thankfulness to a kind and superintending Providence, he saw them one by one disappear in the dark recesses of the forest.

He now bethought himself of rising from his uneasy bed, when lo! a new enemy appeared, in the shape of an enormous rattlesnake, who had thrown himself into the deadly coil so near his face that his fangs were within a few inches of his nose; and his enormous rattle, as it waved to and fro, once rested upon his cheek. A single contraction of the eyelid, a convulsive shudder, the relaxation of a single muscle, and the deadly reptile would have sprung upon him. In this situation he remained for several minutes, when the reptile, probably supposing him to be dead, crawled over his body, and moved slowly away.

"I had eaten nothing," said Lewis to his companions, after his return, "for many days; I had no fire-arms, and I ran the risk of dying with hunger, ere I could reach the settlement; but rather would I have died, than made a meal of the generous reptile."

During the war of 1746, an attack was made on the

settlement around Fort Lewis, at a time when the whole force of the settlement was absent on active duty. So great was the surprise, that many of the women and children were captured by the savages in sight of the fort, though the greater part escaped to the fortress, or concealed themselves in the forests. The fort was occupied by John Lewis, then very old and infirm, his wife, and two young women (French domestics), who were so much alarmed that they scarce moved from their seats. John Lewis, however, placed himself at a loophole, and fired upon the savages, while Margaret Lynn loaded and handed his rifles to him. In this manner he sustained a siege of six hours, during which he killed upwards of a score of Indians, when he was relieved by the reappearance of a party of white troops.

Thomas Lewis, the eldest son of John Lewis and Margaret Lynn, laboured under a defect of vision, which disabled him as a marksman, and he was, therefore, less efficient during the Indian wars than his brethren. He was, however, a man of learning and sound judgment, and represented the county of Augusta for many years in the House of Burgesses; was a member of the Convention which ratified the Constitution of the United States, and formed the Constitution of Virginia; and afterwards sat for the county of Rockingham in the House of Delegates of Virginia.

In 1765 he was in the Virginian House of Burgesses, and voted for Patrick Henry's celebrated resolutions, which looked to war with England and the independance of the Colonies. Thomas Lewis had four sons, who actively participated in the war of the Revolution, the youngest of whom, who is now living, bore an ensign's commission when but fourteen years of age.

Andrew, the second son, is the General Lewis who commanded at the battle of Point Pleasants.

Charles, is the Colonel Charles Lewis who fell at the head of his regiment, when leading on the attack upon the enemy's rear at Point Pleasants.

William, third son, was the Major Lewis of Braddock's defeat. He was an active participator in the border wars, and was a colonel in the American Revolutionary army, in which two of his sons were killed. He was father of Major John Lewis of the Sweet Springs;* also a Revolutionary officer, and maternal grandfather of the writer.

When during the American Revolutionary war of 1776-1783, the British force under Colonel Tarleton drove the Virginia Legislature from Charlottsville, across the Blue Ridge mountains to Staunton, the stillness of the Sabbath eve was broken in the latter town by the beat of the drum, and volunteers were called for to oppose the British progress across the mountains at Rockfish Gap. The elder sons of Colonel William Lewis, who then resided at Fort Lewis (his father having died in 1762), were absent with the Northern army under His Excellency General Washington. Three sons, however, were at home, whose ages were respectively seventeen, fifteen, and thirteen years. Colonel William Lewis was prostrated by an attack of bilious fever, but his wife, who was a Miss Montgomery of Delaware, and a relation of the distinguished General

*Whose daughter Anne Montgomery m. John Howe Peyton—see p 192 ante

Montgomery, who fell on the heights of Abraham at Quebec, with the firmness of a Roman matron, called her three boys to her, and bade them fly to the defence of their native land.

"Go, my children," said she. "I spare not my youngest, my fair-haired boy, the comfort of my declining years. I devote you all to your country. Keep back the foot of the invader from the soil of Augusta, or see my face no more!"

When this incident was related to Washington, shortly after its occurrence, when he was encamped in the snows of New York, defending that province, he enthusiastically exclaimed:

"Leave me but a banner to plant upon the mountains of West Augusta, and I will rally around me the men who will lift our bleeding country from the dust, and set her free."

APPENDIX.

The following Correspondence contains a brief but satisfactory account of the leading incidents and main facts connected with the disastrous campaign of General Braddock, in which General Lewis and one or more of his brothers participated.

JOHN PEYTON,[*] ESQ.,

TO HIS COUSIN

HENRY PEYTON, ESQ.

"Williamsburg, Feb. 25, 1755.

"Dear Cousin Henry,

"You are doubtless aware that an expedition is about to be undertaken against the French and Indians by His Majesty's forces. Governor Dinwiddie invited me to a conference upon the subject of the best route for the army, the means of support, transportation for so large a force, &c., &c., and I arrived here yesterday. I find Williamsburg in much excitement, hurry, and confusion, General Braddock having landed at Hampton five days ago, and reached this city overland; but Commodore Keppel sailed up the river, and cast anchor opposite Jamestown. The sick, of whom there were many, have been landed from the transports, and provided for in hospitals, which had been prepared through the activity of Sir John Sinclair. Those troops fit for duty are encamped on shore, awaiting orders.

[*] This is the John Peyton whose death is mentioned *ante* p. 174.

"One of the most able and enterprising officers belonging to this force, Lieutenant-Colonel Burton, brought to me a letter of introduction from England; and from him —being frequently in his company—I hear much, and greatly interesting information concerning our family and friends in the old country; likewise of the state of political affairs in England. I learn from him that much alarm is felt in London at the encroachments of the French upon His Majesty's possessions in these colonies, and concerning their extensive treaties and alliances with the Indians. Great alarm is likewise entertained for our safety, as well as that of the King's permanent authority in these colonies.

"These apprehensions have caused His Majesty to despatch the force which has just arrived here; and which, together with an auxiliary force to be raised in the colonies, are to operate under the command of General Braddock, who is appointed commander-in-chief of all His Majesty's forces In North America.

"Colonel Burton informs me that General Braddock is a gallant and experienced officer, trained to war, and in every way competent to discharge his difficult and important duties. I called upon the General on my arrival. Likewise I met him in the evening at dinner at Sir John St. Clair's, and the impression he made upon me was favourable, though I have a fear that he does not sufficiently apprehend the difficulties he will have to encounter in the wild nature of our country, and in the Indian mode of warfare. He will, however, have the benefit of the experience and judgment of two promising young men,

Mr. Washington, and Mr. Lewis, who have been a great deal among the Indians, and who understand their savage mode of warfare; as well as the great difficulties of the country. These young men were both at Sir John St. Clair's, and I heard them more than once endeavour to impress these truths upon the British General. Mr. Washington has a dignified earnestness, combined with much modesty of demeanour. Mr. Lewis is more stern and reserved. I discerned some shadow of surprise in the British officer that these young Virginians should assume to offer their advice to him; yet he took it in good part, for indeed what the youths said seemed much to the point.

" February 26.—His Excellency the Governor has determined to bring up the strength of the two English battalions to 700 men each, by enlisting an additional force in Virginia. Picked men will be added to the battalions, and the rest formed into independent companies. On yesterday, cousin Frank Peyton and Mr. Joseph Seldon applied to me to intercede for appointments for them as officers in these companies; and I understand that our young men are all anxious to enter the service, and do duty under the gallant Braddock in what gives promise of being an exciting and successful campaign. Indeed of its perfect success no one entertains the shadow of a doubt.

" Among the troops to be raised by this colony, is to be included one company of light cavalry; and I think Seldon will be appointed to this command, at least I have strongly urged it. He has already comenced recruiting. Lieut.-Col. Burton has promised me to appoint our Frank upon his staff, unless something better turns up for him; so the boys will not be disappointed in their anticipations.

"No general point of rendezvous has yet been determined upon. Yesterday I spoke to General Braddock on this subject, and suggested Alexandria as presenting the greatest inducements. First, because the troops can be taken there by water. Second, it is the best place for clothing and equipping them, and for procuring provisions. Third, it is the nearest point to Fort Duquesne (at which the General will aim) that can be reached by water.

"As soon as this and other points are definitely decided I will advise you.

"It is of the first importance that there should be a hearty co-operation between this and all the colonies as to the plan of campaign. His Excellency spoke to me yesterday about issuing a proclamation and invitations to the other colonies, north and south of us, to furnish men and means. He said that on the part of Virginia he would provide 5,000 men and £20,000 sterling. I suggested to him that it would appear less like dictation (which, by reason of the great jealousy with which Virginia is regarded by many of the younger and less important colonies it is needful not to assume,) if his Excellency would prevail on General Braddock to issue such a proclamation to the country, for that to him, as commander-in-chief, and in the name of the King of England all, including Virginia, would rally. The suggestion seemed to find favour with his Excellency, who said he would consider the same; and might act upon it.

"Mr. Washington called upon me to-day, and informed

me that he would accompany General Braddock in the expedition. He says that his friend, Captain Thomas Lewis, will be despatched with his company to the Greenbrier, there to build and to occupy stockade forts to prevent Indian incursions upon the white settlers in that wild portion of Virginia. Mr. Washington said he had requested the Governor to urge upon me to proceed across the country to Alexandria, and thence westward to Winchester, where I should ascertain what prospect we might have of securing horses, the needful supplies of packs and wagons, together with provisions, &c., for the expedition. He was of opinion that my position as magistrate of the county, and one of the chief landed proprietors, would have not a little weight in securing co-operation, and inquired whether, if prepared to undertake any such mission, I would accompany Sir John St. Clair at once. I pleaded that my age was ill-suited to so severe a journey, and this weight of care; lamenting not the less my other occupations, and entreating that some one more youthful and of greater activity might be selected. Mr. Washington persisted, whereat I consented to consider the matter against such time as his Excellency might see fit to speak to me again.

"Is this Mr. Washington among your acquaintances? If not, I must recommend you to embrace the first opportunity to form his friendship. He is about twenty-three years of age, with a countenance mild and pleasing, promising both wit and judgment. He is of a comely and dignified demeanour, and at the same time displays much self-reliance and decision. He strikes me as being a young man of an extraordinary and exalted character, and is destined, I am of opinion, to make no inconsiderable figure in our country.

"You may expect to hear from me by the next post from here.

"Yours, in haste, but affectionately,

"JOHN PEYTON."

JOHN PEYTON, ESQ.,

TO HIS COUSIN

HENRY PEYTON, ESQ.

"Williamsburg, Va., March 1, 1755.

" Dear Cousin Henry,

" The expedition to the West under General Braddock has assumed some definite shape since the date of my former letter a week ago, and I can now furnish you with the main particulars.

" Alexandria has been fixed upon as the point for assembling one regiment and a part of the artillery; three companies will encamp at Frederick (Maryland), one company at the mouth of the Conecocheague, one at Bladensburg, one at Marlborough; one regiment and the rest of the artillery at Fredericksburg and Falmouth, Virginia, and five companies at Winchester.

" The General has seen fit to make this disposition of the forces for the better convenience of the whole, as they would thus be enabled to converge by their several routes upon Fort Cumberland, and not lumber up the roads in their marches.

"Upon consideration, this disposition of the troops seems to me a most judicious one, and, by reason of the nature of our country, more suitable than my first plan of rendezvous at Alexandria. Also we may hereby avoid the inconvenience which might arise to us from the hostilities now raging between the Cherokees and the Catawbas, the latter the most daring—as you know—of the six nations, and perhaps of all the Indian tribes.

"In the fear that means of transportation may not be at hand, the General and the Governor have requested Sir John St. Clair and myself to proceed to the foot of the Blueridge mountain, there to make contracts with the Dutch settlers for horses, wagons, cattle, flour, &c. We shall set out upon this difficult expedition immediately.

"Meanwhile the Commander-in-Chief will issue a circular to all the colonial governors on this continent, soliciting their co-operation and aid in carrying out his Majesty's plans. Likewise to meet him in conference at Anapolis in April.

(Half a page is illegible here. But on the back—in another hand-writing—are details of contracts made with Governor Dinwiddie for the delivery of eleven hundred cattle in June, July, and August. Also for flour, fish, and bacon; six months rations for four thousand men. Also an agreement with the Dutch, at the foot of Blueridge mountain, who were to furnish fifteen hundred pack horses, and two hundred wagons, to be at Fort Cumberland by the first of May). Then in the original writing of the letter is added:

"Governor Dinwiddie and Commodore Keppel arrived at Alexandria on the 26th of March.

"Yours in much haste,

"JOHN PEYTON."

JOHN PEYTON, ESQ.,

TO HIS COUSIN,

HENRY PEYTON, ESQ.

"Fredericksburg, Va., May 30th, 1755.

" Dear Cousin Henry,

" In our expedition up the country to procure wagons and teams, we were joined by Lieutenant-Colonel Gage and Lieutenant-Colonel Sir Peter Halkett before we reached Winchester.

" I much regret that while we found horses and wagons upon the Virginia side of the Potomac sufficient to remove the troops from Alexandria, none could be procured from the Maryland side to remove those stationed at Frederick, whither the 18th Regiment under Col. Dunbar lately marched. Nor could we secure the requisite number of boats, batteaus, and canoes. These must needs be constructed at Alexandria; and if, in your neighbourhood, there are any men competent for this work, I wish them dispatched there immediately. General Braddock is moved with much anxiety to get his troops away from Alexandria, where no care or punishment can prevent intoxication. But the boats will be of service long after the troops are removed.

"Those troops which had been collected at Winchester were armed there; and Ensign Allen, of the 44th Regiment, was instructing them in their duties.

"I did not return to Alexandria in time for the Council which was held there on the 14th April. It was composed of General Braddock, the Commander-in-Chief, Commodore Keppel, Governors Dinwiddie, Morris, Delancey, and Sharp.

"But on the Occoquan (river) some days afterwards I met Lieutenant-Governor Delancey, of New York, from whom I learned that at the Council General Braddock had announced his purpose to attack simultaneously Crown Point, Niagara, and Fort Du Quesne. Likewise at the Council Mr. Johnston was appointed a Plenipotentiary to the Six Nations; and a speech was prepared for him to deliver in the name of the Commander-in-Chief to the Indians, setting forth that his Majesty the King of Great Britain had sent troops to drive the French from his dominion, and from their hunting grounds, which, in the treaty of 1726, they had given in trust to the English for their (the Red Men's) use and benefit. Also that his Majesty has invested General Braddock with supreme command on this continent, with orders to strengthen the amity which has so long existed between the Red Men and the English, and

238   *Appendix.*

to build forts for the protection of themselves and of their hunting-grounds. That inasmuch as the General could not go to see them himself, he had appointed and dispatched in his stead one of their own Sachems, Mr. Johnston—in whom was invested complete power to speak and act in behalf of the King. And in furtherance of this, the Commander-in-Chief had instructed Mr. Johnston to assemble the chiefs of the tribes for the purpose of a conference, whereat he was to present to them such gifts as had been prepared and forwarded as an evidence of esteem; and to treat with them for the purpose of forming an alliance and lasting friendship; and to tell them that the General would confirm all such agreements as should be entered into between Mr. Johnston and themselves. For carrying out this decision Mr. Johnston was supplied with two thousand pounds sterling, and was instructed to urge upon the Indians the expediency of taking up their hatchet against the French.

"On my way to the western country to procure means of transportation and supplies for the army I went as far north as Frederick (Maryland), and there I met with Mr. Franklin, of Pennsylvania, who was greatly interested in the success of the expedition. He promised to use his best endeavours to procure five hundred horses for the use of the army. While I was there, General Braddock arrived on his way to Fort Cumberland, which place he reached on the 10th of May, with the 44th and 48th Regiments, the former under the command of Lieutenant-Colonel Sir Peter Halkett.

"The artillery arrived a few days later. So likewise did

the horses and wagons which Mr. Franklin had promptly dispatched from Pennsylvania.

" In haste I remain yours ever affectionately,
"JOHN PEYTON.

"P.S.—Despatches have just arrived from Fort Cumberland. By a letter from F., I learn that some apprehension is felt by our Virginian officers that the rigorous discipline of the English army will be found unsuited to our hardy and independent volunteers from the frontier. These men, who have grown up in the vicinity of the Indians and are as bold and rugged as the monntains which have given them birth, have learned to protect themselves after a fashion of their own, and already feel themselves more competent to guide the English than to be led by them.

"The troops are marching from Fort Cumberland in a north-westerly direction, and my recent expedition to the wild regions of the South Mountain enables me in some sort to picture amazing difficulties to be surmounted by an army. For, in the first place, they will have to cut for themselves a road through the primeval forests which clothe the lofty ranges of the Northern Apalachians, to ford the mountain torrents, to scale the steep gorges, and to encamp in the lair of the bear and the wolf. Young Washington and Lewis, who are already acquainted with those wild regions, will here have an opportunity of commending themselves to the favour of the Commander-in-Chief by affording him the advantage of their experience. Indeed, I feel full confidence in the valour and prowess of our Virginian officers.—J.P."

CAPTAIN FRANCIS PEYTON TO HIS MOTHER.

"Monakatuca Camp, 16th July, 1755.

" My dear Mother,

" I would have written to you from Winchester before we commenced our march, but Mr. Hite, who was returning to Alexandria, promised he would let you know all you desired concerning me; and how full of business I and all the rest of us have been, preparing to move through the wilderness in the direction of Fort Duquesne.

"We have found provisions very scarce. Our men, too, are most difficult to control, all of them having lived on the frontier in a state of freedom and independence, which has rendered them unwilling to submit to authority. The majority of them seem to have joined the expedition from pure love of excitement, regarding it as something in the nature of a buffalo hunt. They shoot away their ammunition after game, notwithstanding it is strictly against orders. Nor do they even take precautions for their own safety, but contrary to orders fall behind and straggle, and are generally disposed to rebel against authority. Indeed, they indulge in many irregularities, which greatly shock the English officers, who are accustomed only to well-trained and disciplined armies. And this our (Virginian) officers see and lament, knowing that in the circumstances by which we are surrounded they cannot be repressed by the same means which are used in Europe. To-day we have had a melancholy evidence of the recklessness of these mountaineers, for during our march four of them were shot while loitering, and scalped by the Indians. A company of sharpshooters was scattered in search of our stealthy foes, but in vain; it was impossible to overtake or find them. Such sad experience as this will soon teach these reckless men that safety lies alone in obedience.

"We have encountered every kind of difficulty during our march from Winchester. Frequently we have had to cut our road through the pathless forest, and to let our baggage and wagons down steep precipices by ropes and pulleys. Our horses also have become exceedingly thin and feeble; for as this wild country is entirely without enclosures, we cannot let them loose at night, or they might stray away, or be captured by the Indians, who hang constantly upon our path. Consequently our horses, being but half nourished, can now scarcely pull our wagons. This obliged us as early as the beginning of last month to send back two pieces of cannon. This occurred when we reached Martin's Plantation. From that place we crossed the Alleghany Mountains by a steep and rocky ascent of over two miles, and amidst scenery of surpassing grandeur. At the foot of that range we crossed a wild and beautiful stream called Savage River. On the 24th June we crossed the Yoxhio Geni River, and though we left Martin's Plantation on the 13th June, the difficulties of our march were so great that we had accomplished only that distance, 23 miles, in twelve days.

"At the Yoxhio Geni River we came so suddenly upon an Indian camp that we captured an old warrior, who was unable to escape with the speed of his light-footed companions. He informed us that 170 of his comrades, all fighting men, had been with him: notwithstanding that but a few minutes had elapsed, they had all disappeared so mysteriously that not one of them could be discovered, though a party of our light troops were despatched immediately in pursuit. Among them were several Frenchmen: and of this we needed little proof, many trees being stripped, so that they might write upon the bark all kinds of scurrilous language, threats, and bravadoes. Although we could not discern any of the French or Indians, they lay in ambush close around us; and on the next day three of our men were shot and scalped by them. Occasionally we saw some of their painted faces in the woods at a distance, and during the night they repeatedly attempted to reconnoitre our camp.

"Every mile of our march was now bringing us rapidly into their country, and into the midst of them; and during the next night we came upon another of their camps, where fires were still burning. Here also were the trees stripped by the French, and many insolent sentences written or carved upon the stems, and some drawings were made of the scalps of our men who had been killed two days before. After quitting that camp we came upon a more open country, and our roads were less difficult, for there was no undergrowth. Those woods were composed chiefly of white oak timber, in place of the chesnuts and laurels which covered the ridge we had cut our way through.

"On the 4th July we camped at Thicketty Run, and General Braddock sent forward some Indian scouts towards the French fort, to procure intelligence. These scouts returned on the 6th, bringing with them a French officer's scalp. The Frenchman had been out shooting within half a mile of the fort, when they killed him.

"I have now, my dear mother, given you a kind of diary of the most striking events that have occurred to us up to this point of our march. I regret that time will not allow me to be more full and particular in my descriptions. It would please me to give you a more lively account of this truly savage country, and of some sublime spectacles produced by the effect of the setting sun among the lofty peaks of the mountains by which we are surrounded. But the courier who is to take this to Fort Cumberland will leave in five minutes. Therefore I have barely time to send my love to all my dear kinsfolks, and to sign myself,

"Your dutiful and affectionate son,
"FRANCIS PEYTON."

"Great Meadows, July 13, 1755.

"My dear Mother,

"Never did I undertake to write a letter when so overwhelmed with grief and disappointment. Our expedition has failed! Our commander is dead! Our noble General Braddock! He died this day from his wounds. Alas! who could have anticipated such a disaster—such an extraordinary and disgraceful defeat as that which we have sustained on the Monongahela river.

"I will endeavour to give you some connected account of our military operations since the letter I wrote you from Monaktuca Camp.

"Well, my dear mother, after leaving that spot our whole army arrived at the Monongahela river and crossed it on the 9th July. It is a bright and beautiful stream of about 200 yards width at that part; but varying both in width and depth; sometimes rattling playfully over the rocks which form its bed, and sometimes flowing silently under the rugged roots and branches which stretch half across it. It was very shallow where we crossed, as I suppose it generally is during the dry season. We crossed it in the first place full of hope and confidence; we have recrossed it in shame and confusion! I was acting as adjutant of Colonel Burton's regiment. According to his orders I had formed in columns of companies to the right of the main force, which was on the opposite side of the stream. The scouts reported the French and Indians in great force near at hand; therefore our whole army was drawn up in line of battle. The General issued the order to advance. We did so; and had not proceeded 500 yards when we heard quick and heavy firing along nearly our whole line. In order to ascertain the force of the enemy, and their exact position, General Braddock called a halt; and directed that our regiment, with the vanguard of 800 men, should move forward to reinforce the pickets and reconnoitre the enemy's position. Lieutenant-Colonel Burton placed himself at the head of the regiment, and advanced in gallant style. We had proceeded hardly one quarter of a mile, when we came upon our pickets retreating in confusion, bringing terrified and exaggerated accounts of the enemy's force. This threw the vanguard into disorder, which disorder quickly spread among our men. Suddenly we beheld our savage enemy advancing upon us; for we had not been able before to see them through the thick forest in which we were. The confusion greatly increased, and our men were now falling wounded and dead in all directions from the brisk fire which the Red Skins opened upon us. Colonel Burton and the other officers exerted themselves to the utmost to induce the men to stand their ground, and return the enemy's fire; or to advance upon, and dislodge them from their hiding-places. But in vain; panic-struck they retreated upon the baggage in the utmost precipitation and confusion, and had hardly come back to it before the French and Indians attacked us in this position. Every man of us must have been destroyed, and I should never again have addressed a letter to you, my respected mother, had it not happened that four pieces of cannon were stationed in reserve at that point. These were promptly manned, and chiefly by officers, who thus succeeded in keeping back the foe. Notwithstanding we held them thus in check, a murderous fire was kept up upon us and our whole line. Nearly all of our horses and drivers were killed, and those who were not, fled; for still our treacherous foe could not be seen through the trees and thick undergrowth: and excepting the road which we had cut, there was no opening whatever.

"General Braddock seeing that it was necessary to advance and dislodge the enemy, rode forward with his staff to the front. He endeavoured to reanimate their courage, and induce them to advance, dashing forward through the thick forest to show his indifference to danger. But, oh! that I should have to write it—he failed, and while thus exposed was shot down, dangerously wounded. So also was the brave Colonel Burton, while many officers were killed. This greatly increased the panic, and in spite of our efforts to retire in good order, we found it impossible to control the men, who fled. The only regiment in which there was any steadiness was the 48th. At the head of this, Colonel Burton, notwithstanding his wound and loss of blood and consequent prostration, endeavoured to advance. He was aided by Colonel Washington and Colonel Lewis who had rallied around them a body of Western Virginians. These men protected themselves by the trees while they fired—after the fashion of the Indians—and thus prevented an advance of the enemy. But for all that their efforts were futile, the 48th refused to advance, but stood firing helplessly at the forest trees behind which the enemy were concealed, until they had expended all their ammunition; after which, in spite of the officers, they broke and fled towards the river in the wildest confusion; many of them throwing away their arms and accoutrements. In spite of being thus forsaken by the panic struck 48th, the brave Western Virginians whom Colonels Washington and Lewis had formed behind the trees—after the Indian mode of fighting—retreated, but in order, from tree to tree, loading and firing as they drew back, upon such of our snake-like enemy who showed themselves in advancing. The Colonial Volunteers thus prevented pursuit, and saved the remnant of the British army from destruction. Meanwhile, Colonel Washington had had the wounded General Braddock carried to the rear, and carefully tended.

"The whole of our retreating force recrossed the river in safety; and on the 11th we reached Gist's Plantation, where our wounded were attended to, and the army rested for a short time. We then continued our retreat to Rock Fort, near Colonel Dunbar's, and thence to this point which we have only reached this evening.

"The whole retreat has indeed been conducted by Colonel Washington, whose remarkable talents have gained the general confidence of the other and senior officers. His principal and most efficient aid in this humiliating task has been Captains Andrew and William Lewis, of Augusta, (county) who have lived all their lives on the frontier, and perfectly understand the Indian character. Thus, my dear mother, you will perceive that to the volunteers of my native Virginia, we entirely owe our escape.

"During our flight (for nothing else can it be properly

called), we have suffered exceedingly; but those who had escaped injury, seeing the great anguish of those who had been wounded, have been manly enough not to complain.

"I have been with the wounded general during some or other portion of each day. He endured agonizing pains of body, and, if it were possible, still greater anguish of mind at the failure of the campaign. Indeed, it appeared to be a relief to him that he would not survive so grievous a disaster. He entertained the hope that his king and his country—since he had laid down his life in their service—would shield his memory from any unjust or ungenerous imputations connected with this most fatal enterprise.

"It is a source of much pride and pleasure to me, to witness how rapidly our friend and neighbour, Colonel George Washington, has grown in the estimation of all, by his wisdom and prudence; and by the great ability he has displayed in extricating the army from an unfortunate and dangerous situation. He is spoken of in terms of praise by all—both colonial and English officers, and particularly by General Braddock, whose last breath was drawn while sounding his praise, and exhorting obedience to his orders. Though Colonel Washington does not belong to the British army (for, like myself, he was a a volunteer in this expedition), has, indeed, never been to England, or received any regular military training, he has the faculty of inspiring confidence in officers and men alike: particularly—if any can be singled out—is he admired by Colonel Burton. All agree that in future campaigns against the Indians, it will be better to conduct them under officers born and bred in this country; and not by persons despatched from England, however competent the latter may be considered. They cannot understand America so well as the natives, who have already learned the way to fight the savages around them. And in this age the Indian craftiness has been quickened by their French allies.

"I will write to you soon again; and give you further particulars; unless there be a strong prospect of my meeting you soon at Fredericksburg.

"Our sick and wounded are suffering intensely from the heat of the weather, and from the mosquitos, gnats, and other insects; also from the want of proper medicines and supplies, ours having been for the most part lost during the flight.

"The scenery of the country though which we have passed since leaving Winchester has been wondrously grand: widely differing from that around Fredericksburg, which is comparatively flat. But I have no heart now to describe it in this hour of our defeat, humiliation, and disgrace.

"With my dutiful love, I remain, your affectionate son,

"FRANCIS PEYTON."

THE END.

London: Printed by A. Schulze, 13, Poland Street.

Just ready in One Volume, demy 8vo., Price 16s.

THE

ADVENTURES OF MY GRANDFATHER.

BY

COLONEL LEWIS PEYTON, L.L.B., F.R.G.S., &c.

Author of " The American Crisis." A historical and statistical view of the State of Illinois, &c. Late Chief of Staff to General Douglas B. Layne of Virginia.

JOHN WILSON, PUBLISHER,

93, GREAT RUSSELL STREET, LONDON, W.C.

ON SALE

BY JOHN WILSON

A large collection of old books on Biography, Topography, Metaphysics, Poetry, Rare Quaker Tracts, English History, including some rare Civil War Tracts, Books with plates by Bewick, Cruickshank, and Blake, Early Wood Cuts, Shakespeariana, &c., &c.

Books bought and exchanged. Works not in stock procured on reasonable terms.

Post Office Orders payable at 38, Great Russell Street.

In 2 volumes, post 8vo. Price 21s.

THE AMERICAN CRISIS;

OR,

Pages from the Note Book of a State Agent during the Civil War.

BY

JOHN LEWIS PEYTON,

Bachelor of Laws of the University of Virginia, Corresponding Member of the Wisconsin State Historical Society. Fellow of the Royal Geographical Society of Great Britain, &c. Late Lieutenant-Colonel Commanding 18th N. G. Chicago.

NOTICES OF THE PRESS.

"These volumes are compiled from the notes of the Author, who was at one period an accredited agent in Europe for one of the late Confederate States. The incidents commence from the outbreak of the war, and there are numerous authentic facts and data given which will throw light upon many circumstances connected with the long struggle between the Northern and Southern States. The descriptions of scenes visited, the reflections on social subjects, and the statements connected with the secret history of the war acquired by the Author in his official capacity, are of the highest interest and importance."—*Sunday Observer.*

"The American Crisis rises to the rank of a voluminous state paper. Colonel Peyton's work is destined, we believe, to be the text book for posterity, as far as regards the political questions opened up by this Civil War, the most gigantic conflict the world has ever witnessed. The Author gives very spirited sketches of the preparations for the fight, and the interest taken in them by the veterans of the South. . . . Throughout he proves his sound common sense and perfect mastery over the difficult science of political economy. . . . Colonel Peyton has told the history of the American Civil War, its commencement, progress, and ultimate close, with precision, and with considerable historic care. He has woven with the main thread of his story, too, so many strands of minor interest, so many sketches, and so many glances at English and American domestic and country life, that each succeeding year cannot fail to add to its value as a photograph of its own times."—*Jersey Express.*

"We have seen no work upon the American Civil War, more entertainining and thoroughly readable than that by Colonel Peyton. The style of which is terse and vigorous."—*The Cosmopolitan.*

"Some of the most interesting portions of these charming volumes contain a summary of Colonel Peyton's experiences as well in the political, as in the literary world. His sketches are graphic and beyond all controversy life-like. We commend these volumes cordially and conscientiously to perusal, and we err if their circulation be not extensive. Their Author was, we believe, some two or three years ago resident for a little while amongst us, and has since been for a longer season domesticated in Jersey. It is not improbable that he may, ere long, once more be a visitor to the Channel Islands, and in that case we are sure that we may promise him for ourselves, and equally confident that we may prognosticate for him from our neighbours, a very hearty welcome. What Sidney Smith called "stress of politics," has driven many a honoured exile from freedom or for conscience sake, upon our shores, but surely none more worthy of our esteem than this intelligent and gallant gentleman of whom—his enemies themselves being judges —the very worst that can be said must be, ' Victrix causa Diis placuit, victa Peytoni.' "—*Guernsey Star.*

" Colonel Peyton's book is half a narrative of his reminiscences of the Great Civil War, or rather of his personal intercourse with its chief actors, both military and political, and half a description of his experiences in England, and his impressions of English society. He exhibits considerable skill in blending his adverse feelings towards Jeffreson Davis (whom he regards as a common-place politician and not a genius at all) with the necessary amount of attachment for the Confederate cause. Some of the chapters which he devotes to his personal observations while in this country will be read with interest, and portions of them with amusement. Of course he does not like Mr. Cobden or Mr. Bright. Of Lord Russell's appearance and manner he speaks with a contempt which is not wholly unmerited, but ill-becomes a panegyrist of Mr. Alexander Stephens of whose outer man he has given the most unflattering of descriptions. But he is at all events impartial in his satirical judgments. When he presents what is on the whole a very uncomplimentary portrait of Mr. Roebuck he is perhaps more true to life, but he makes a poor return for much zealous service."—*Daily Star.*

"This subject is unrivalled in importance to Americans, and a very arduous one with which to deal; the interests involved are so manifold, and the questions connected with it so complicated that it requires a master-mind to do it justice. Colonel Peyton has taken very elevated views of all these great questions. We have rarely met with a writer who combines so much impressive earnestness with so much sound sense and masculine depth of thought."—*Gazette.*

"Here we pause, reluctantly;—the extreme interest we take in the political portion of Colonel Peyton's most valuable and instructive work, has induced us to discuss somewhat at large what we may venture to entitle "Sentiments proper to the present crisis," and that with reference as well to England as to America. It is not, however, to the statesman or historian alone that these volumes will be interesting. Their Author has mingled largely in the best society on either side of the Atlantic, public and private life in both hemispheres, with their leading warriors, orators, statesmen; artists and men of letters, have come as a matter of course under his notice, and are sketched ably by his graphic pen;—he is in turn a Hogarth and a Watteau, as eccentricities and absurdities, graces and amenities are to be delineated. Nor is graver information wanting; his work is replete with historical anecdotes, valuable statistics, and sound and apposite reflections upon subjects of contemporary or social interest."—*British Press.*

"These volumes are full of grace of thought, and purity of feeling."—*Spectator.*

"It is curious to see with what contempt this gentleman of high birth and solid position, looks down on the mushroom leaders of secession. Most of these men are sketched by Colonel Peyton in sharp and biting acid."—*The Athenæum.*

"The American Crisis is a highly entertaining work, and one in which the reader's interest will seldom or ever flag. Many of the sketches are hit off with much skill and effect."—*B. Herald.*

"The earlier portion of Colonel Peyton's work draws a lively picture of the feelings which prevailed in the south, and especially in Virginia, during the first months of the war. The sanguine advocates of Secession were full of hope and animation, predicting a speedy triumph of their cause, which should force Massachusetts itself to return all fugitive slaves, and place the prosperity of New England at the mercy of the Southern Confederacy. Colonel Peyton's second volume is devoted, for the most part, to life in England. He gives us particulars about hotels and lodging-houses, describes our railway management and railway carriages; sketches some of our great men: tells us about our dinners, our evening parties, our country houses, and our manner of living in them, in point of fact, is communicative to Englishmen; and the other, on England for the use of Americans. But we can imagine many reasons which may have made it more convenient for him to treat together the two countries which have been connected by his own experience. He is not at all a fatiguing writer to follow; we may read with tolerable care what he has to tell us about America, and may then proceed with undiminished energy to glance at his remarks on a subject which, after all, has an interest for most of us—ourselves."—*The Guardian.*

LONDON, SAUNDERS, OTLEY AND CO., 66, BROOK STREET, W.

CPSIA information can be obtained
at www.ICGtesting.com
Printed in the USA
LVHW092142191219
641188LV00008B/65/P